Roman myth
Future Art Publisher

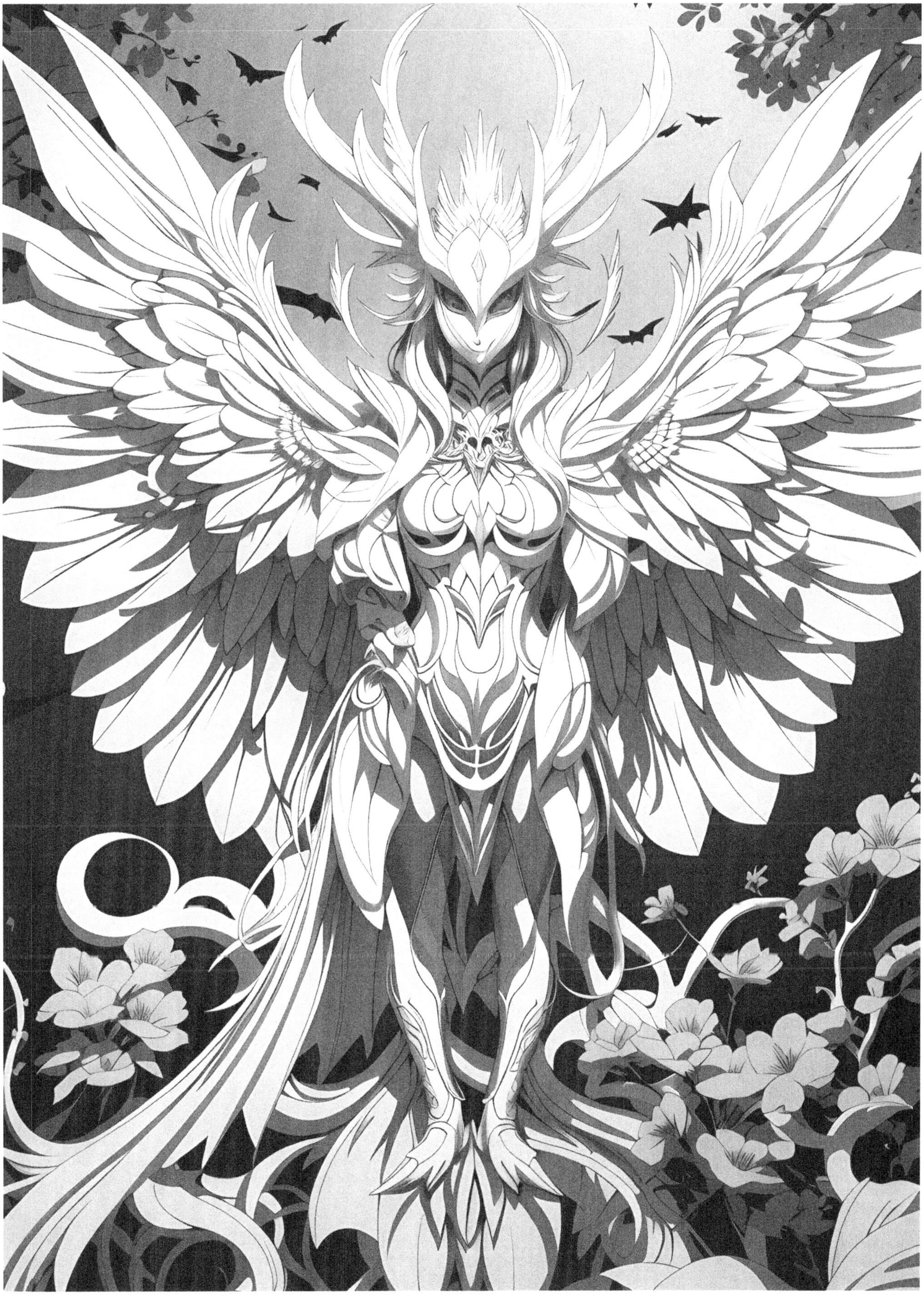

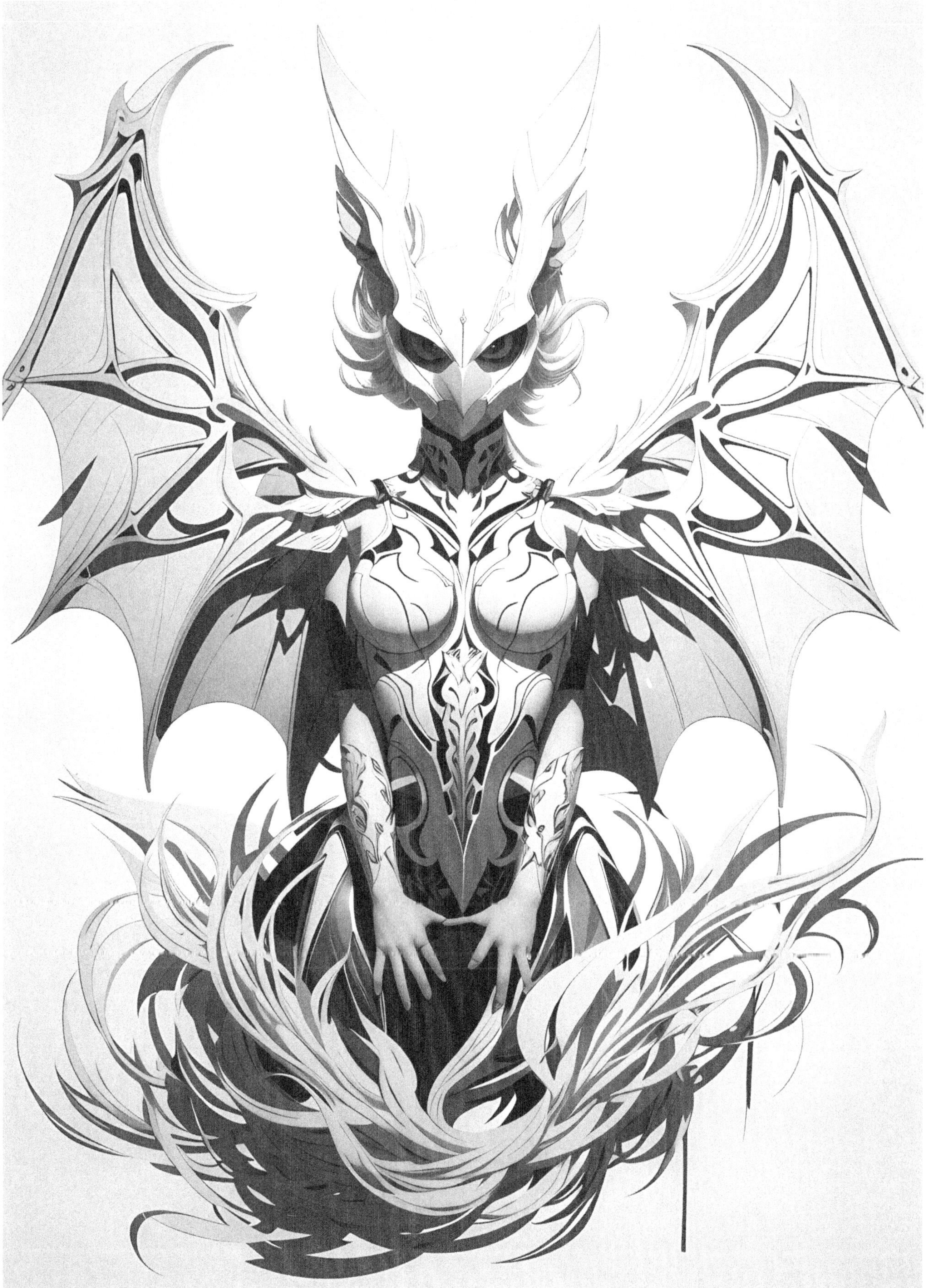

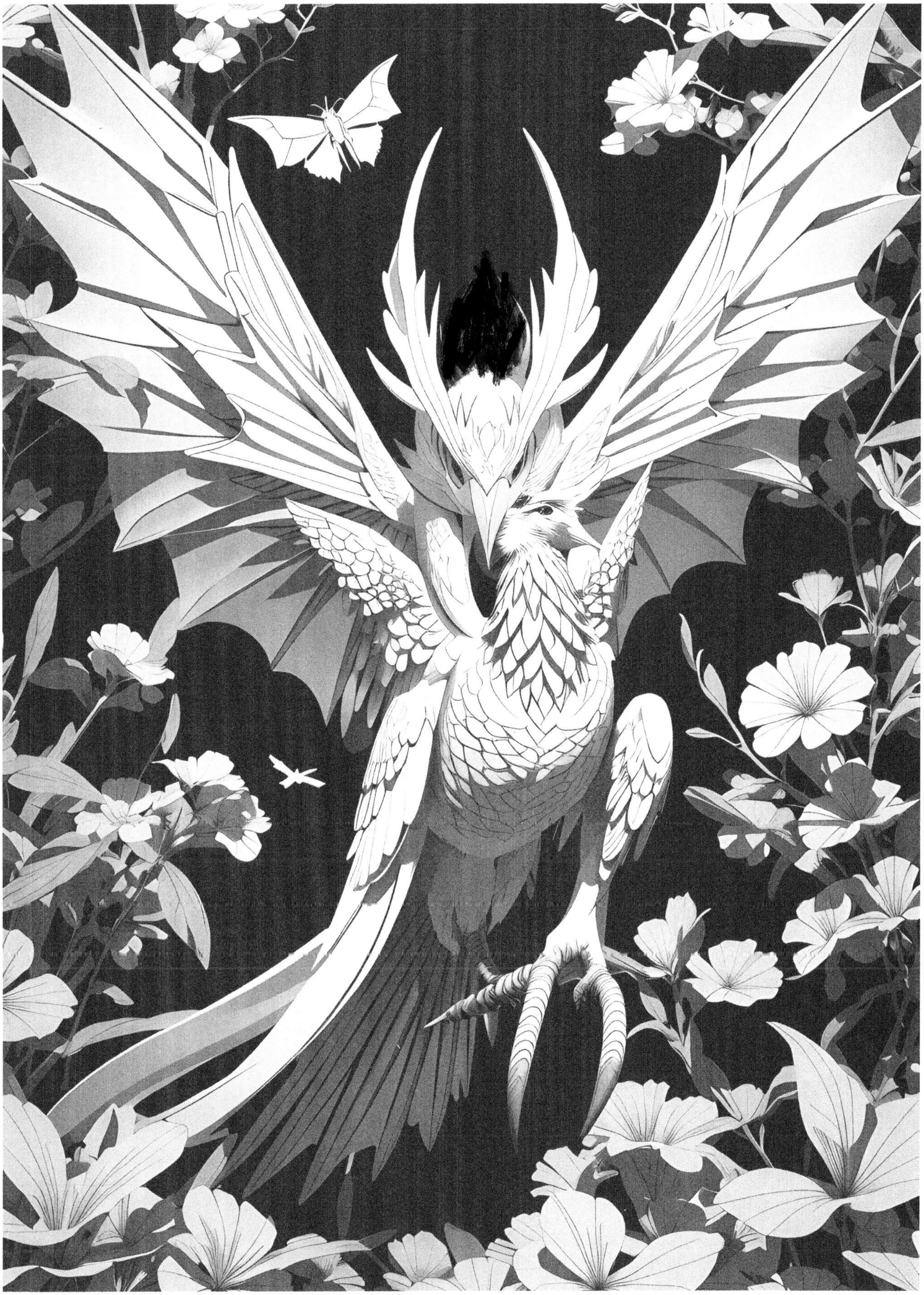

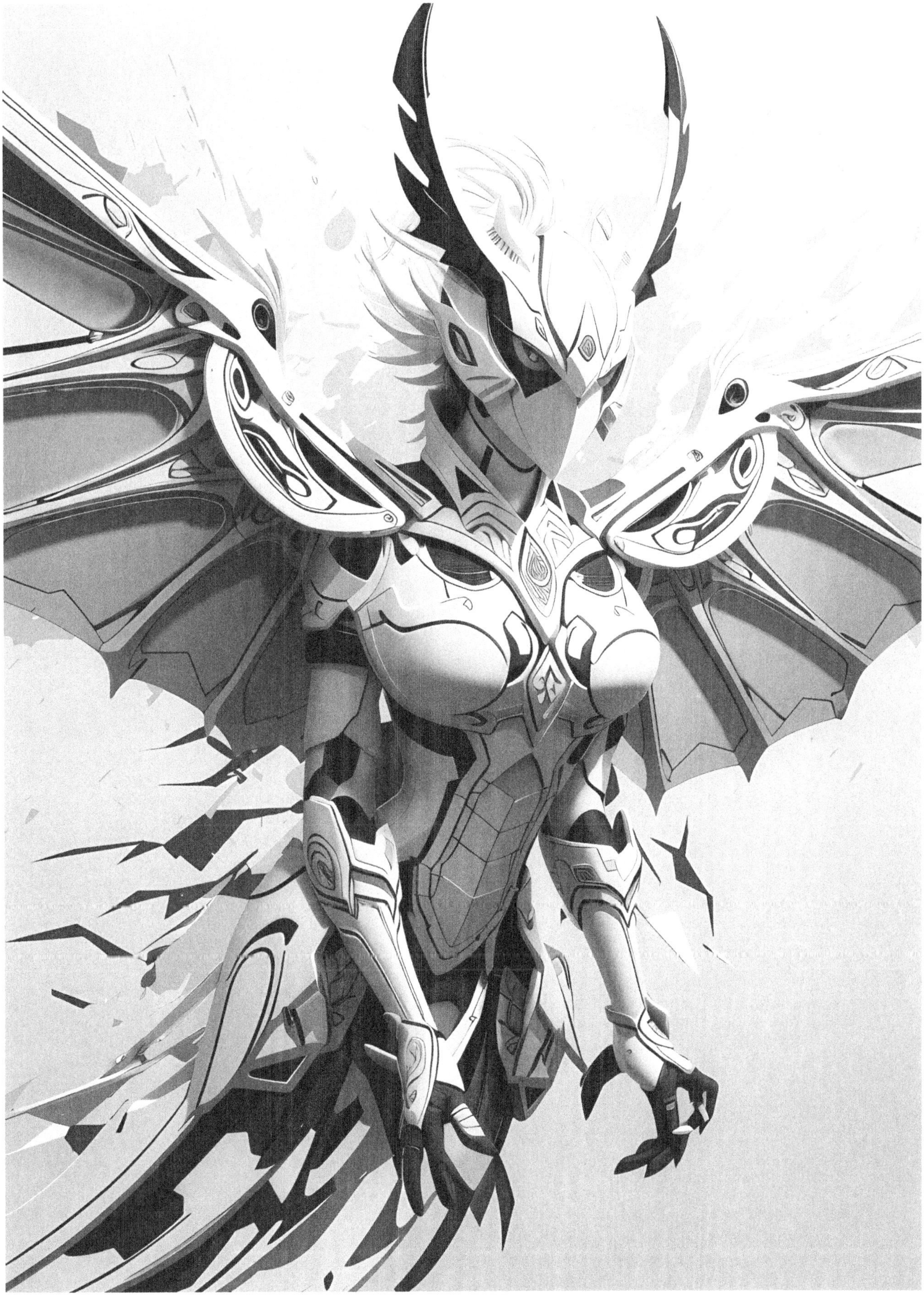

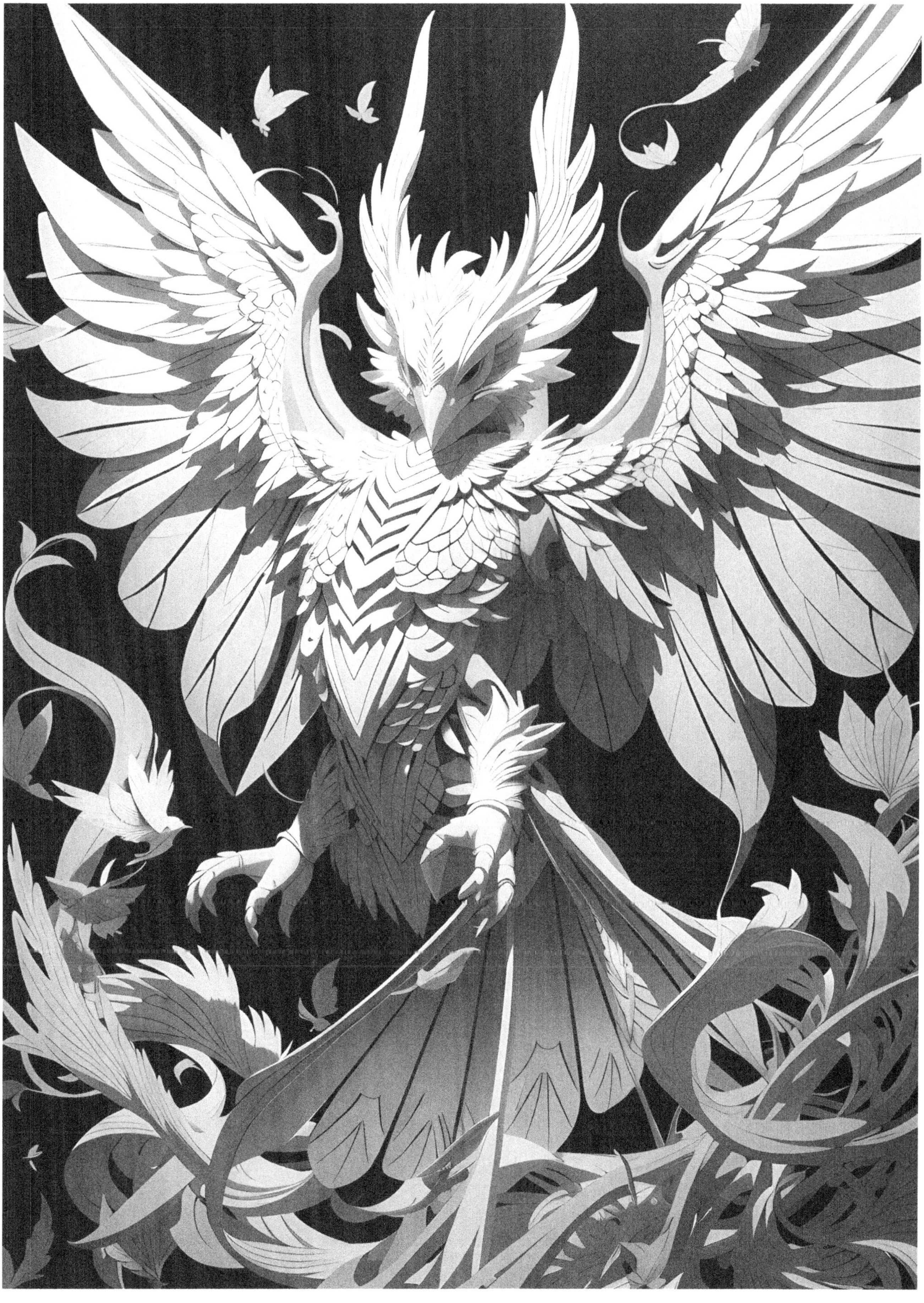

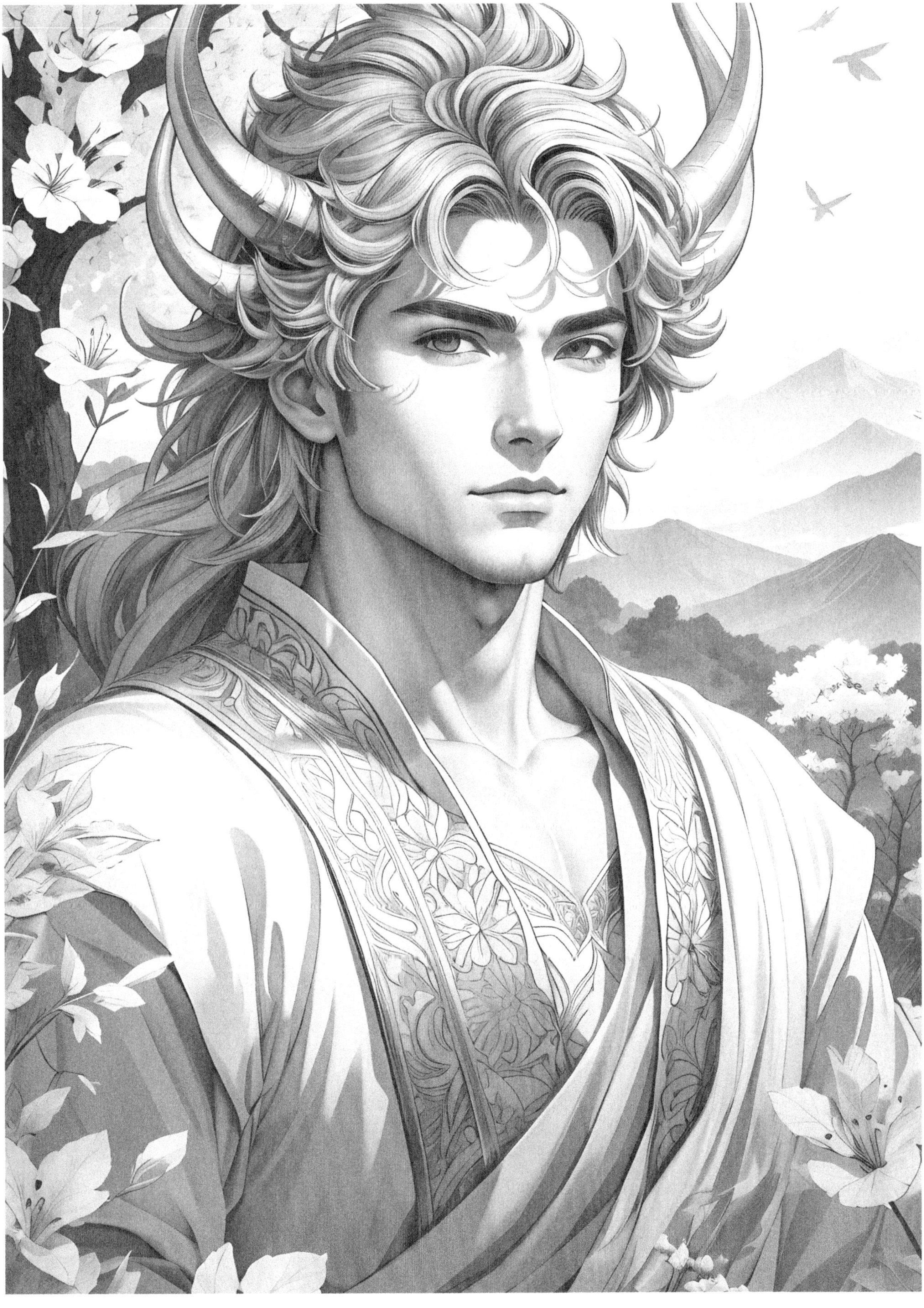

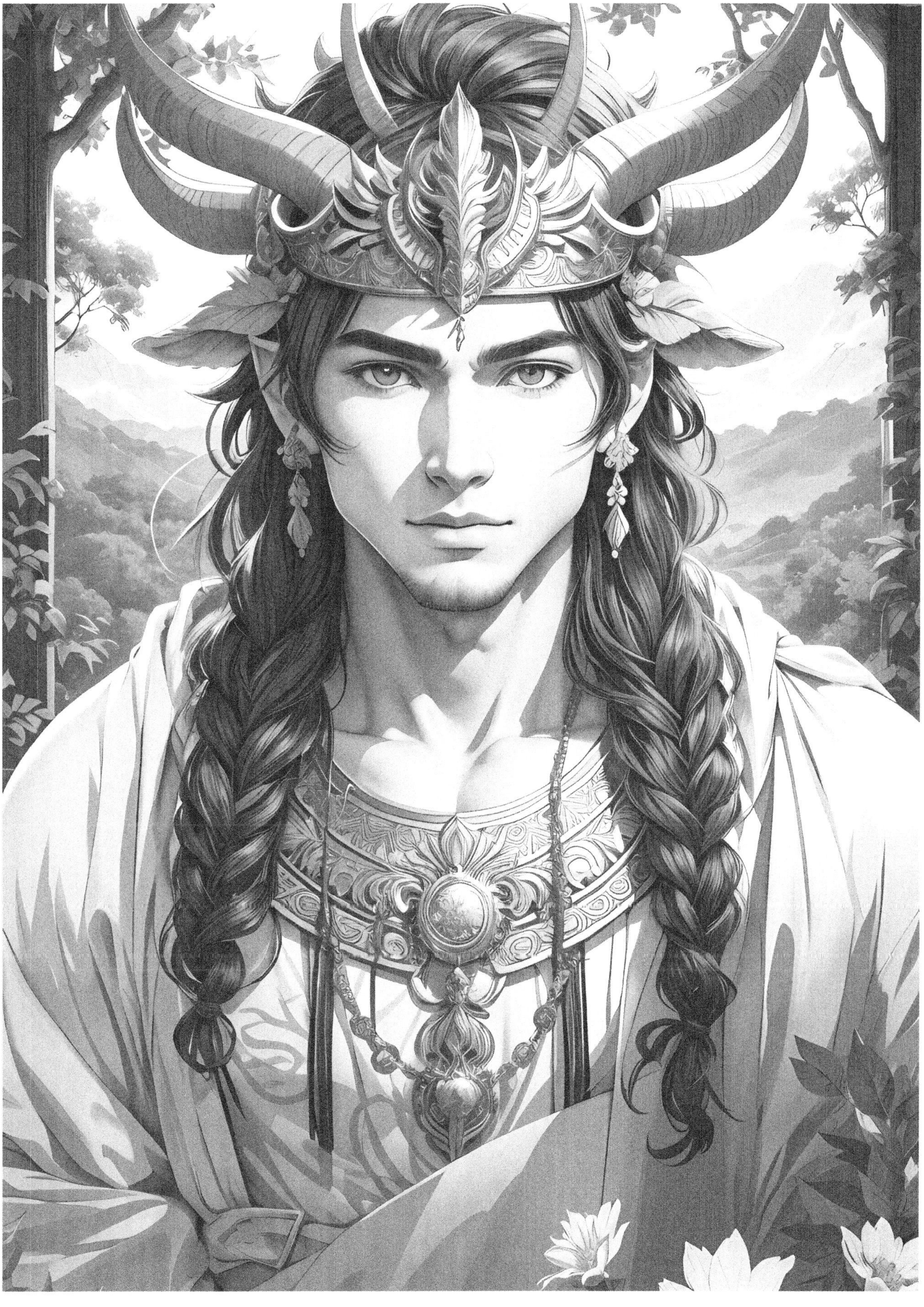

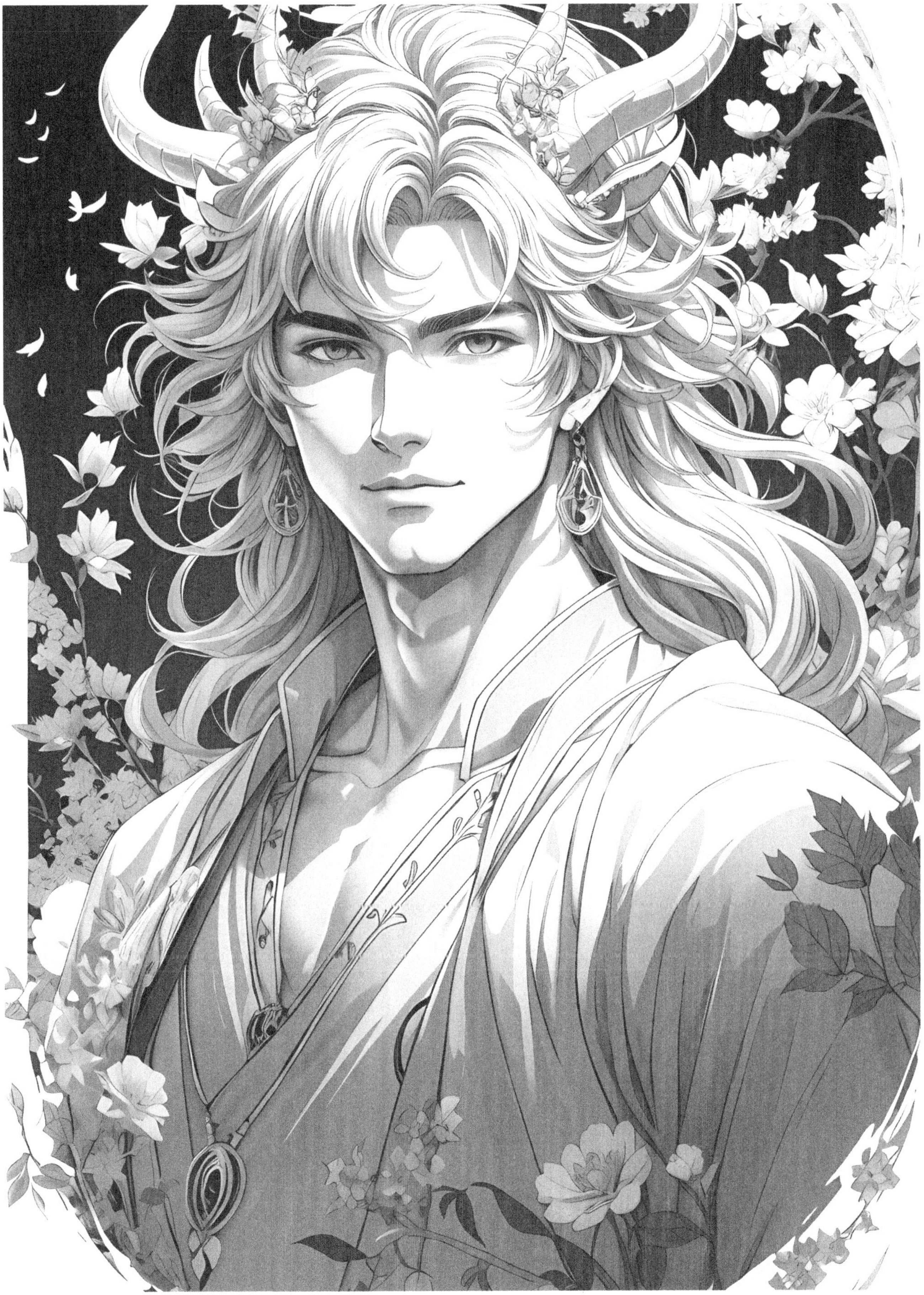

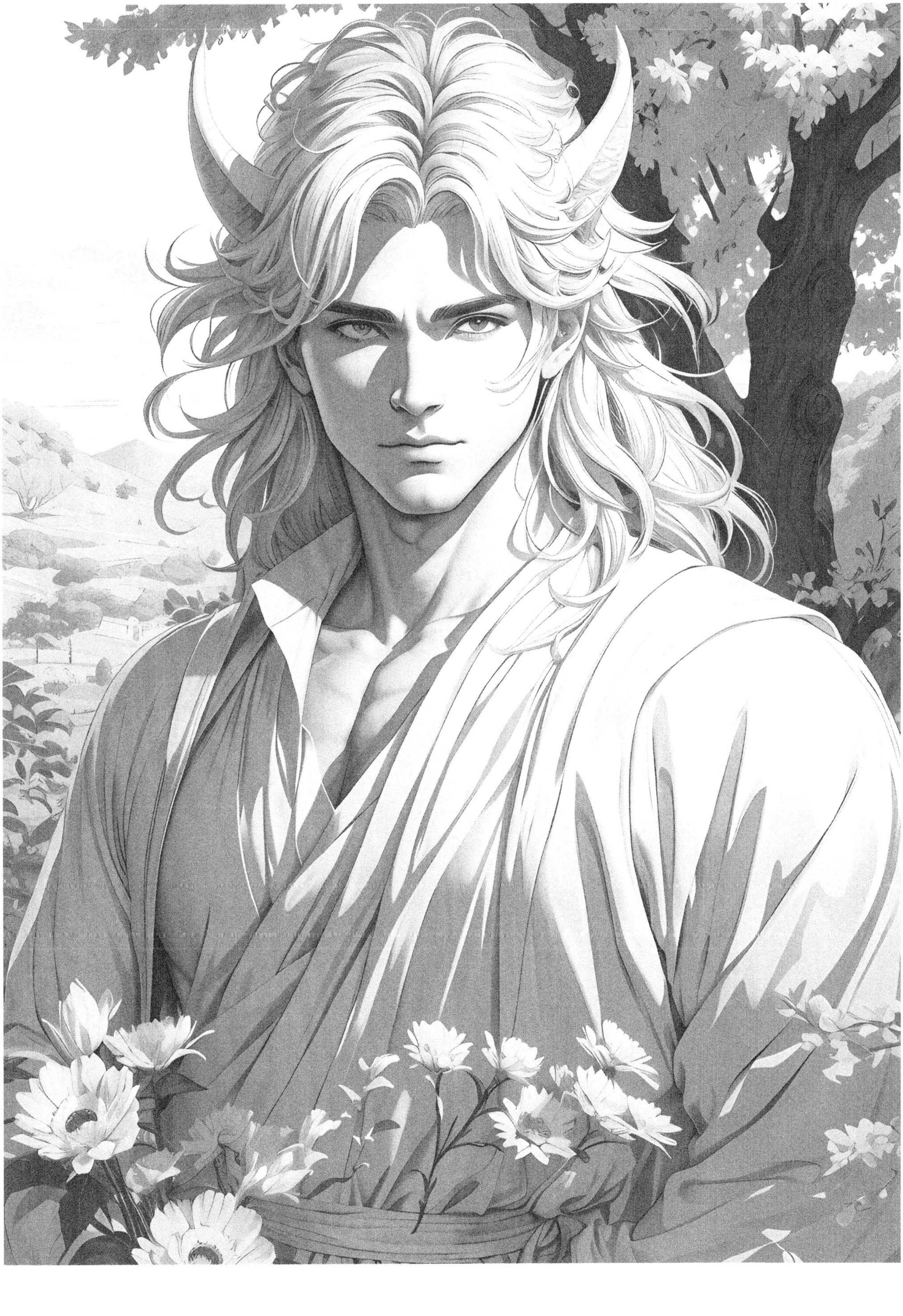

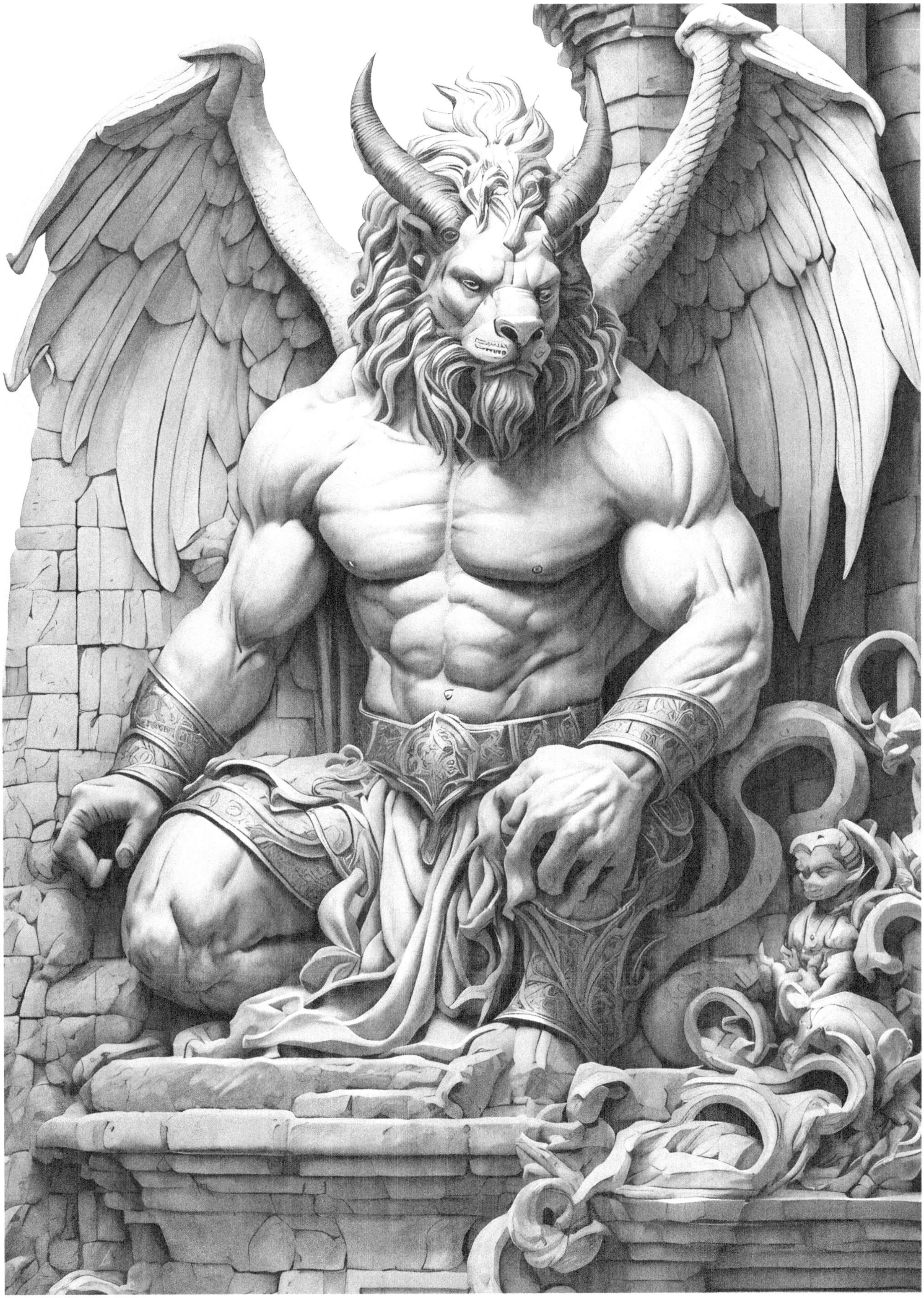

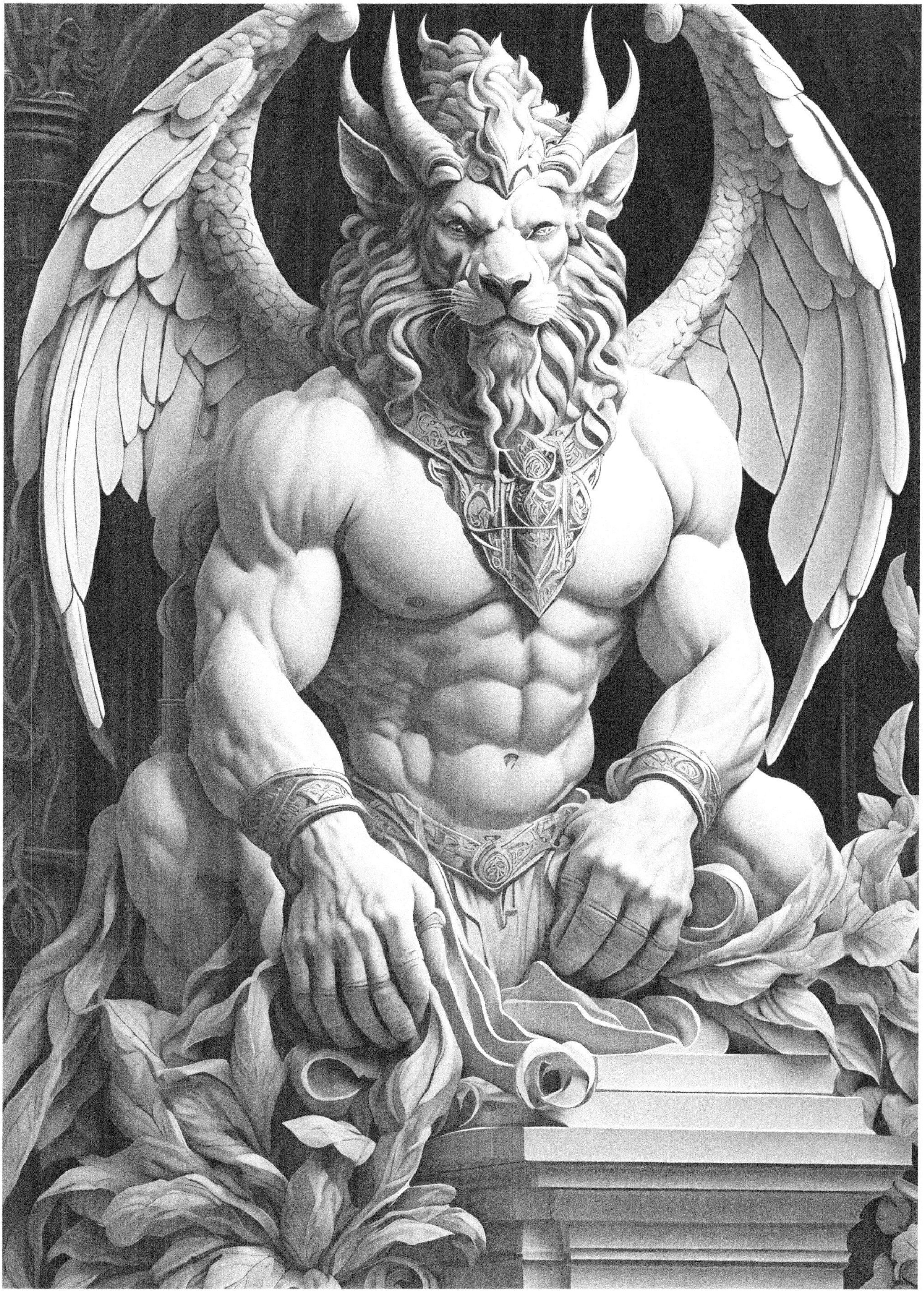

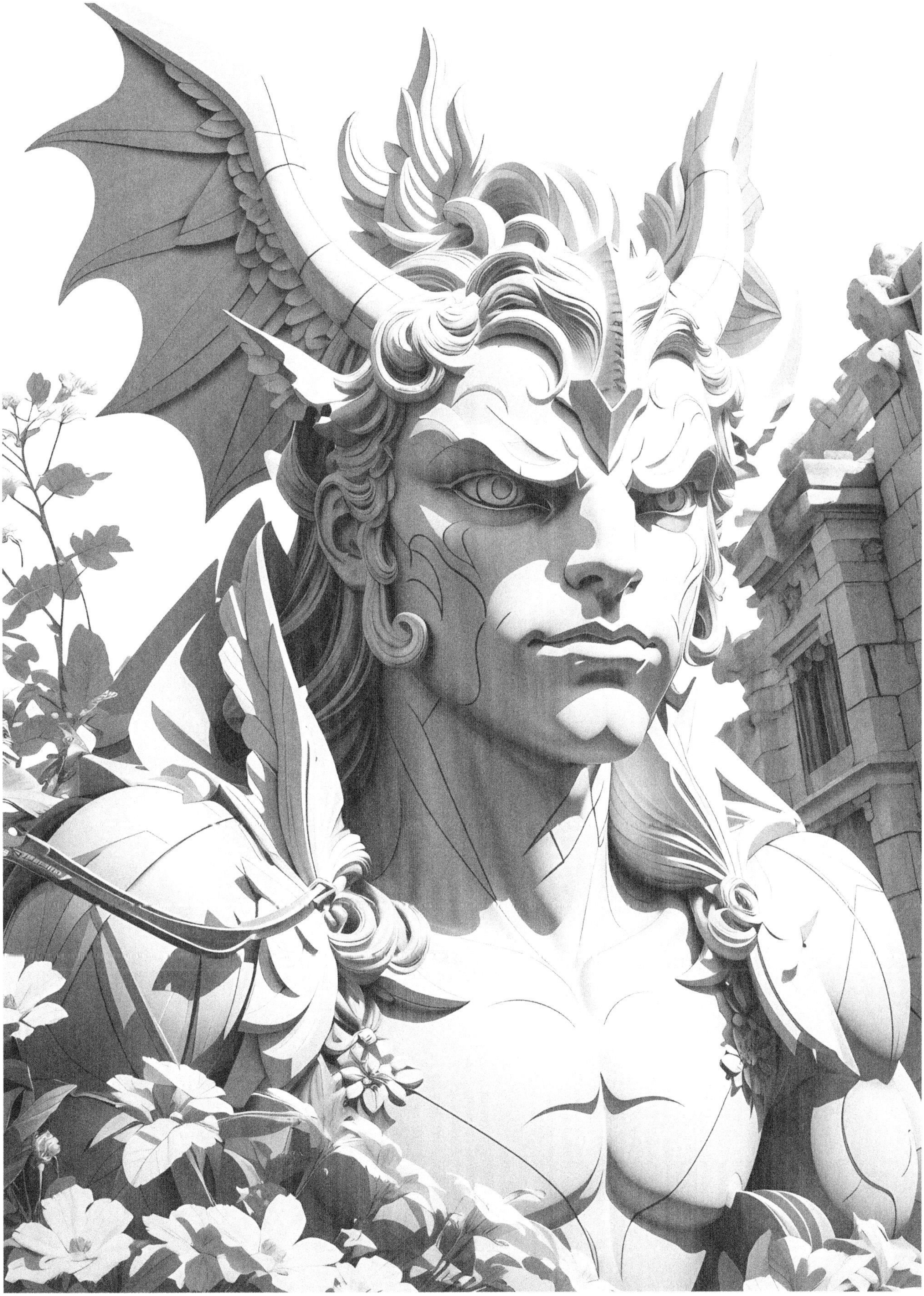

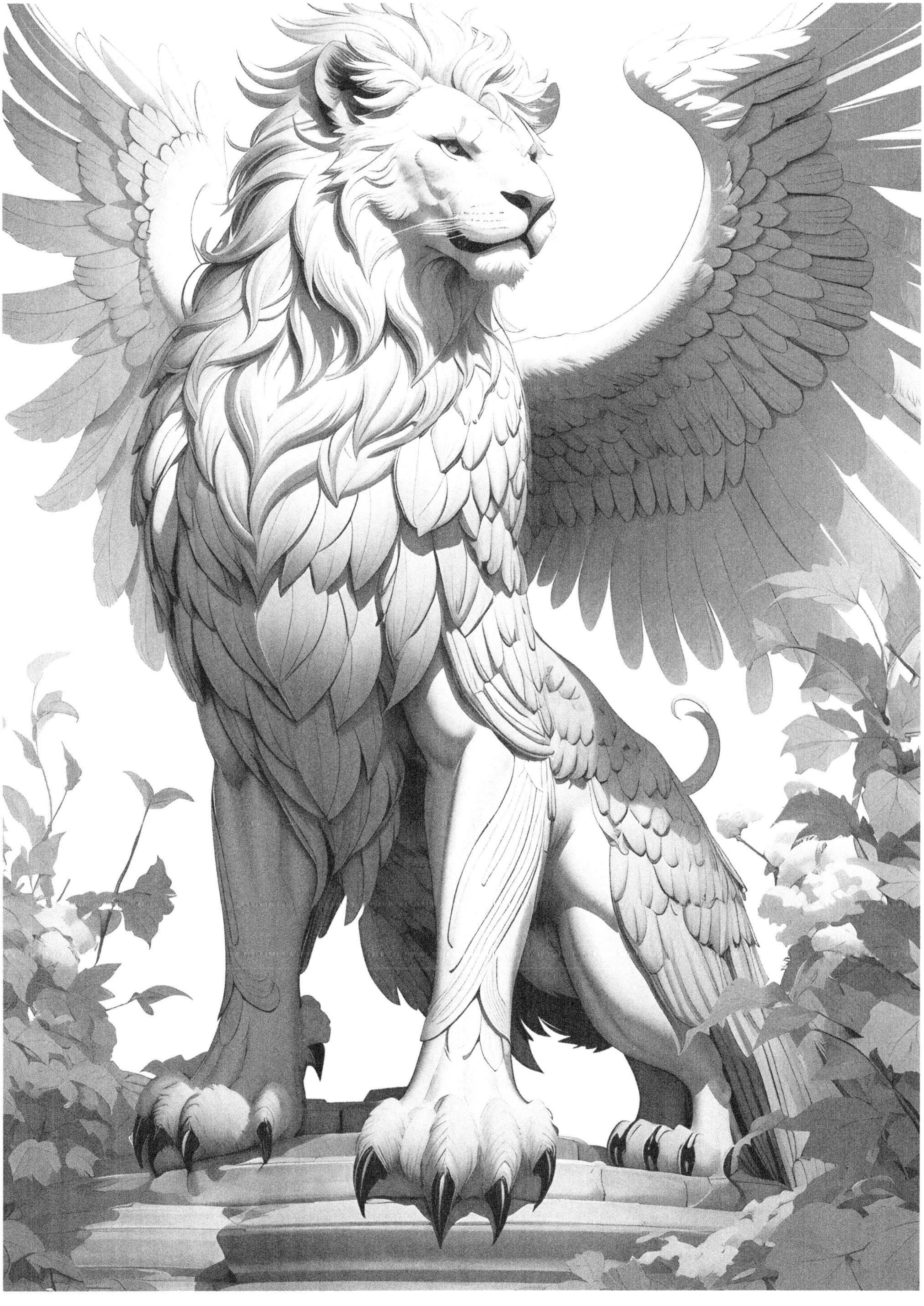

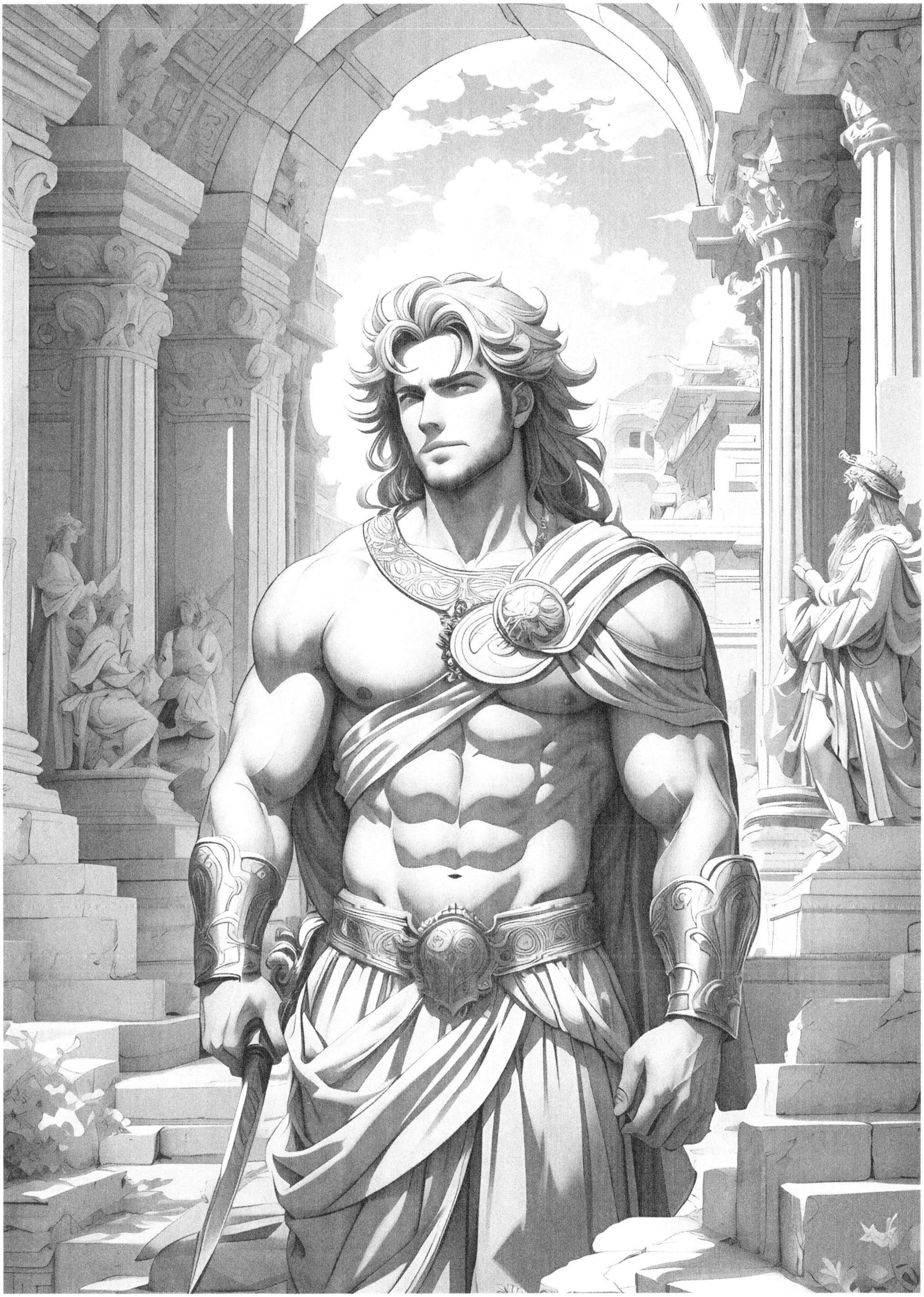

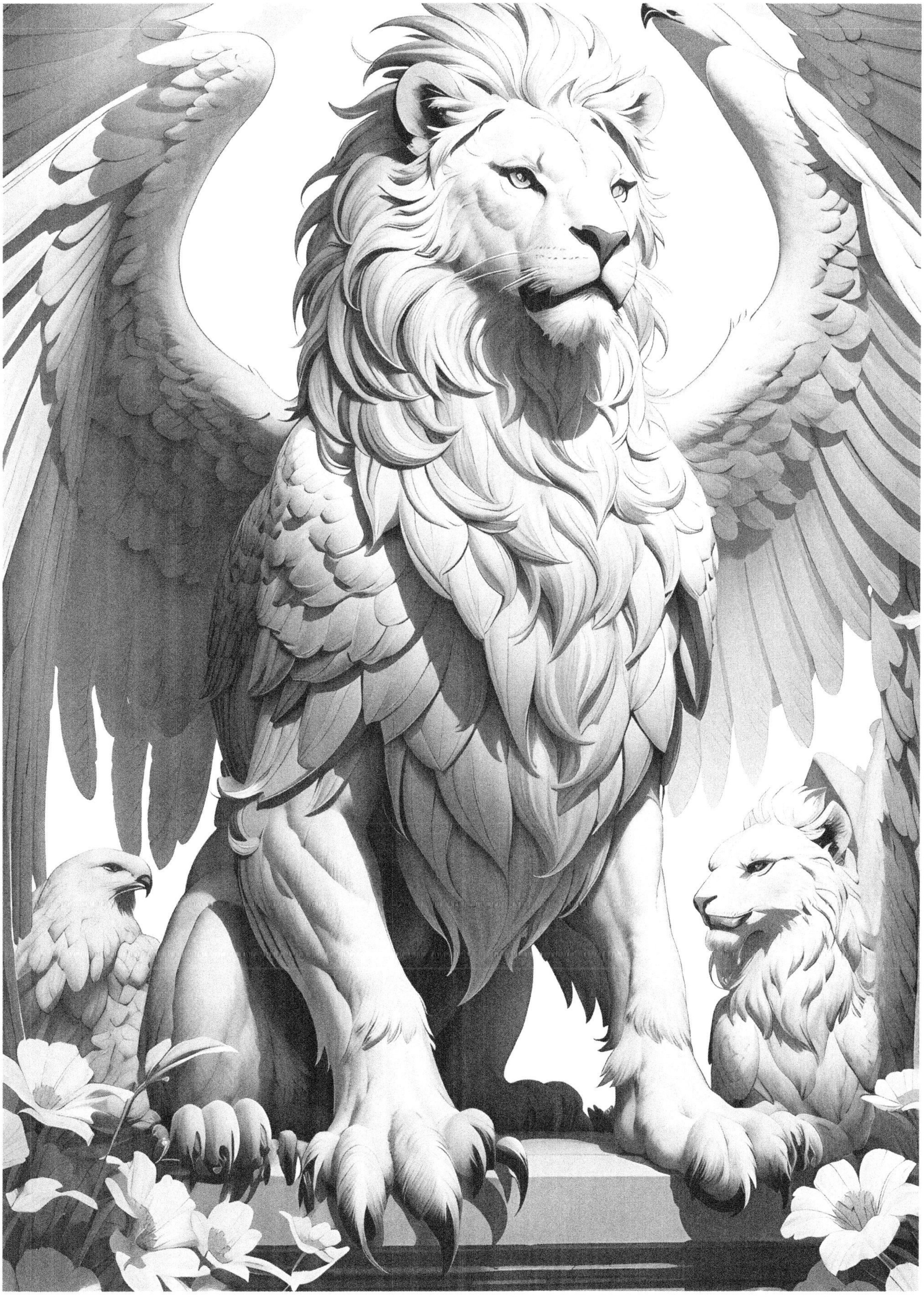

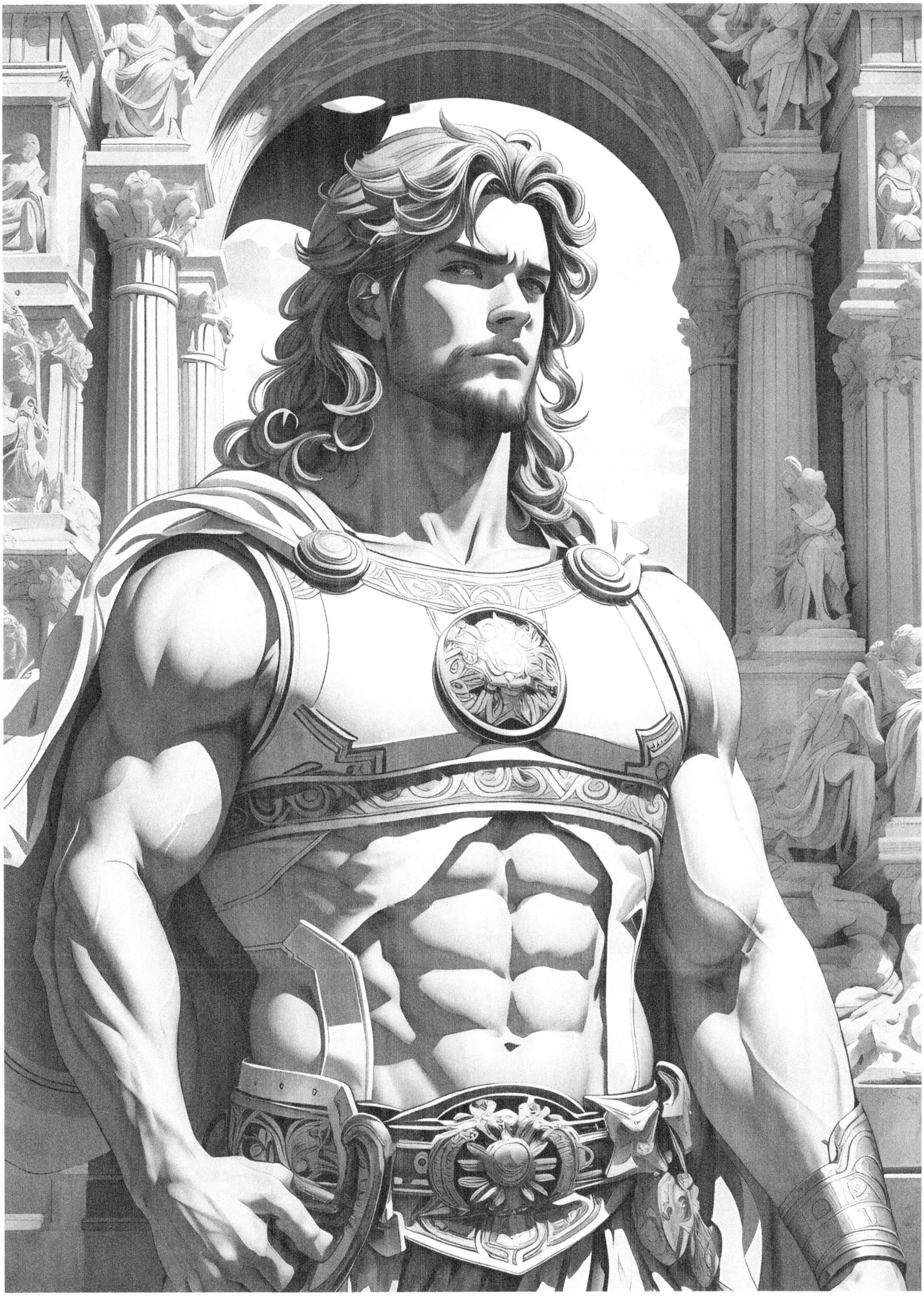

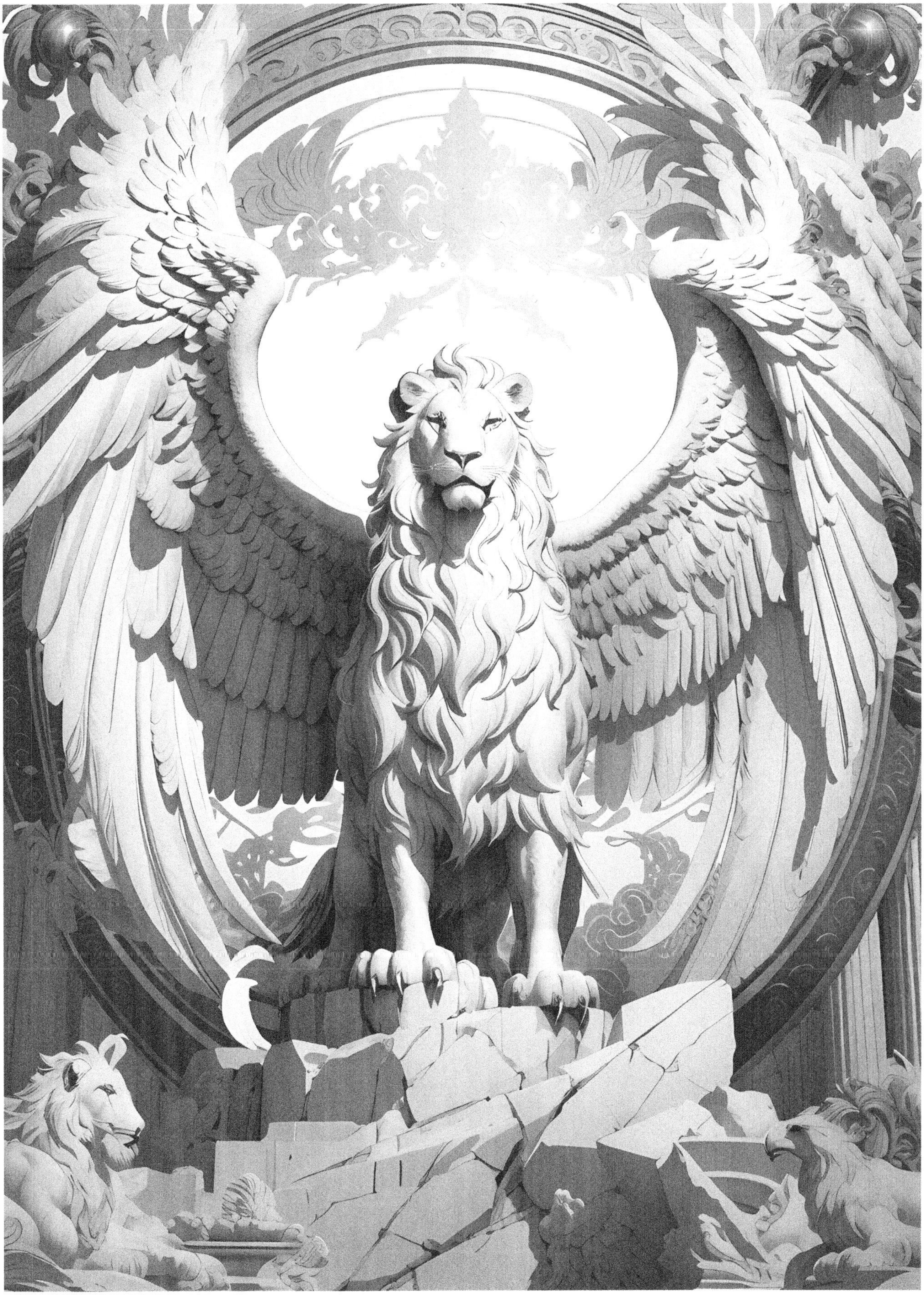

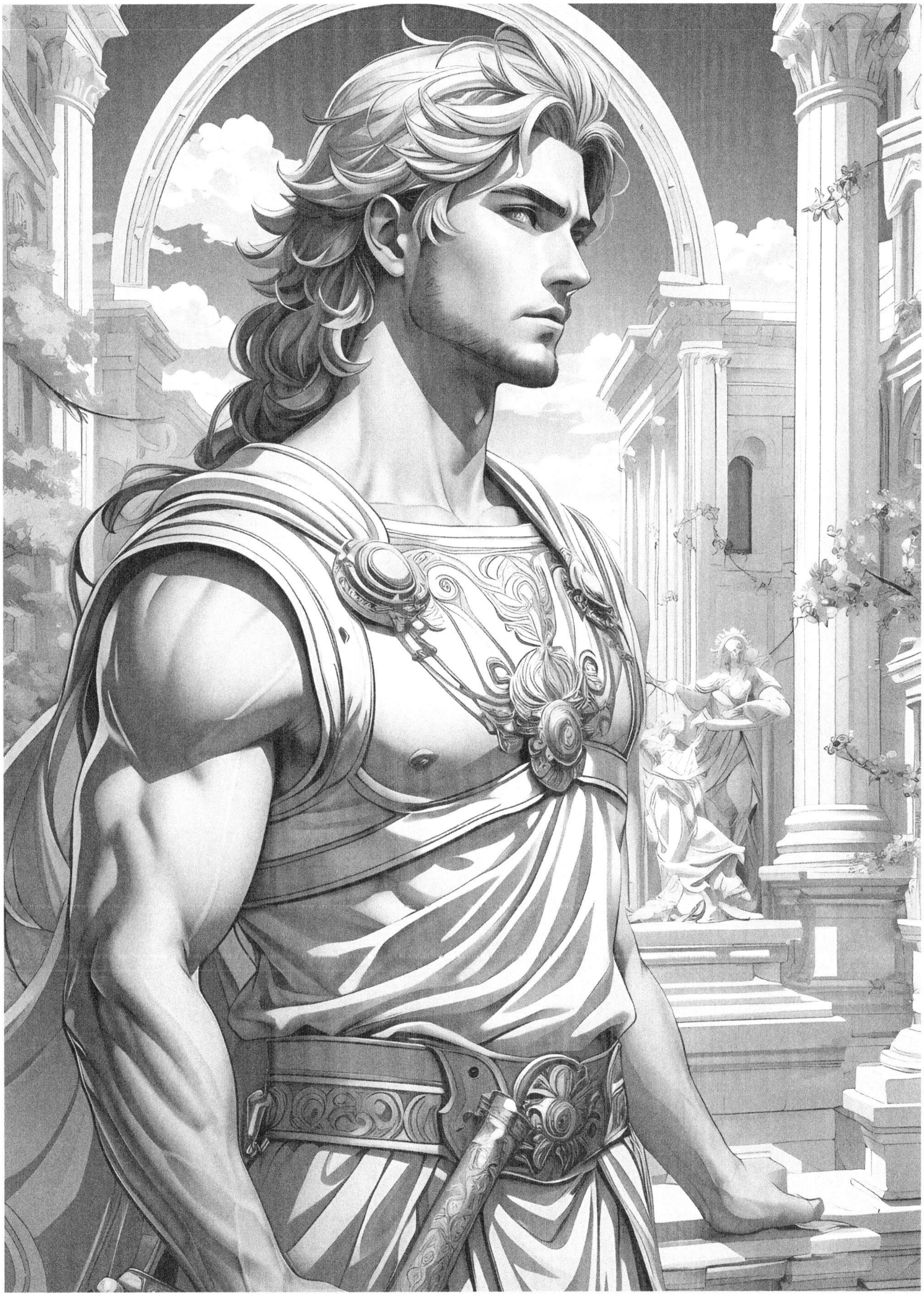

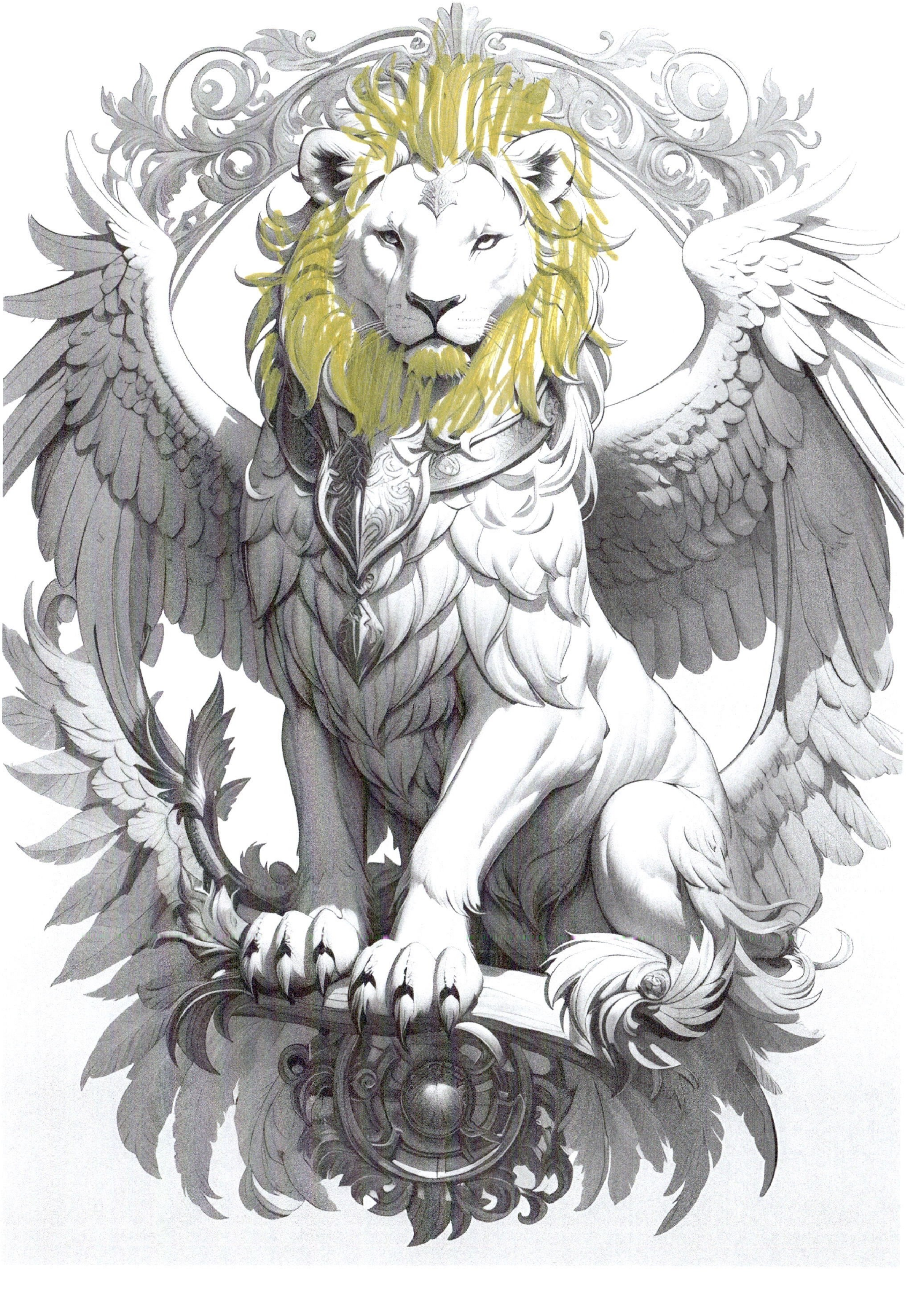

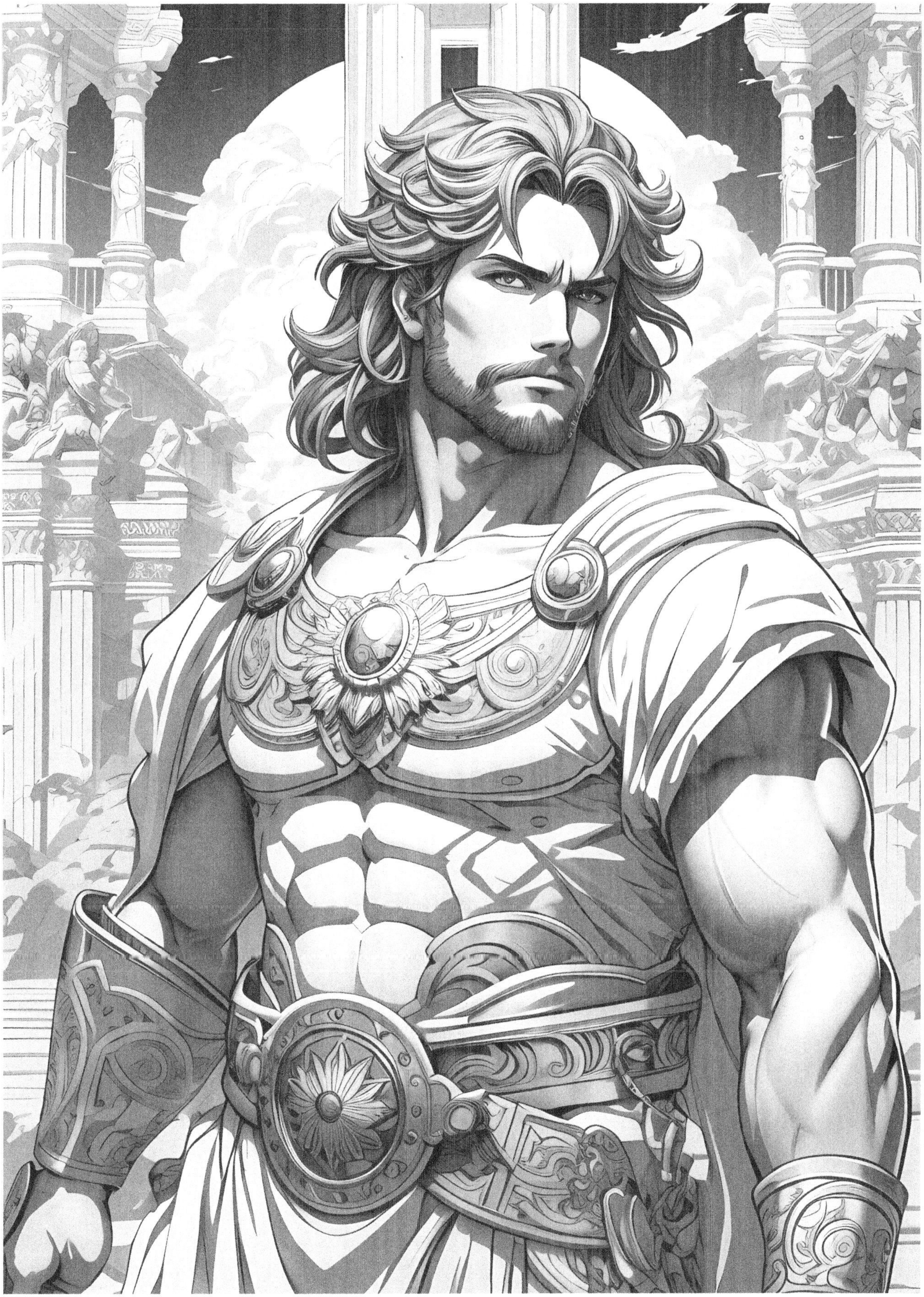

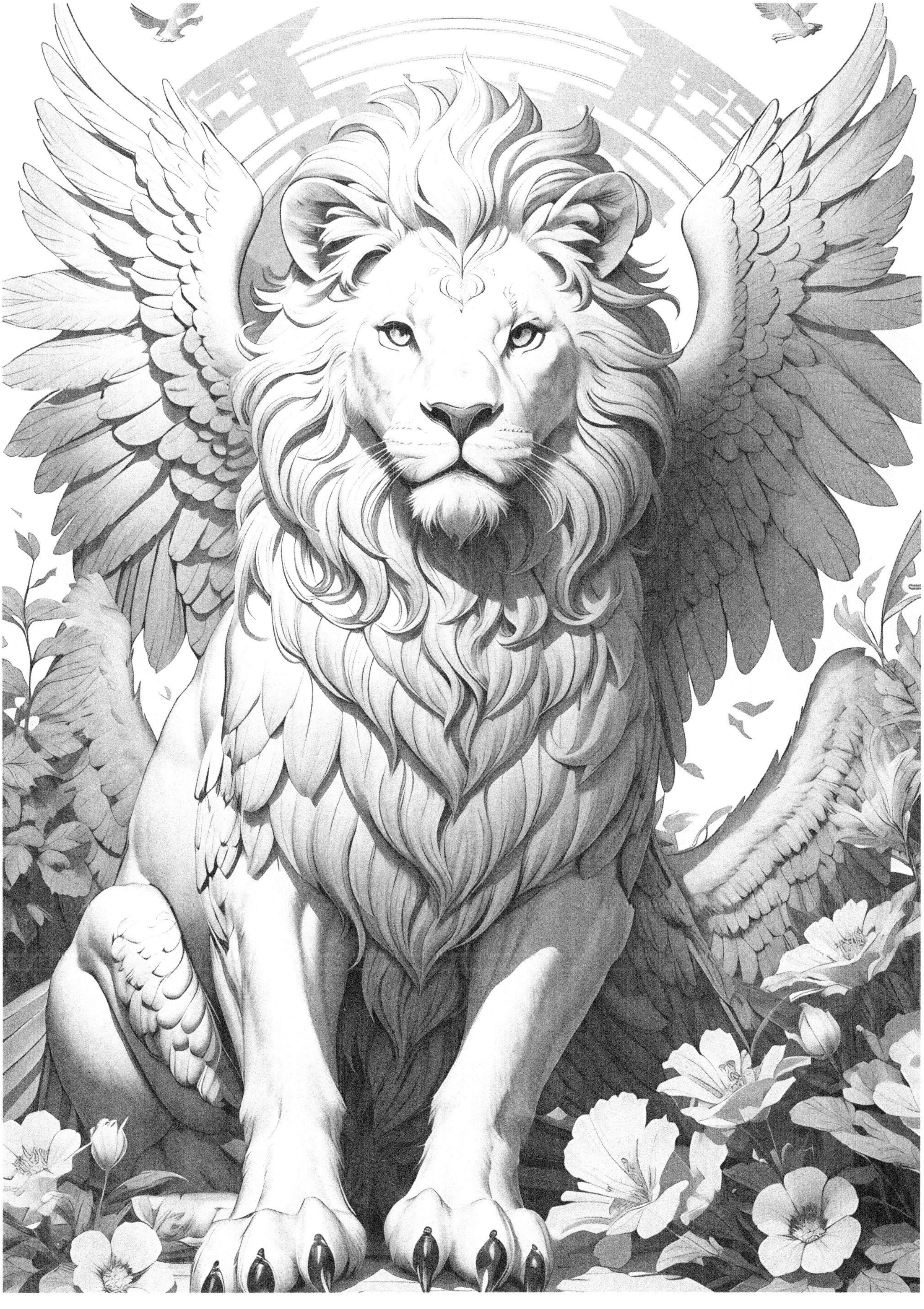

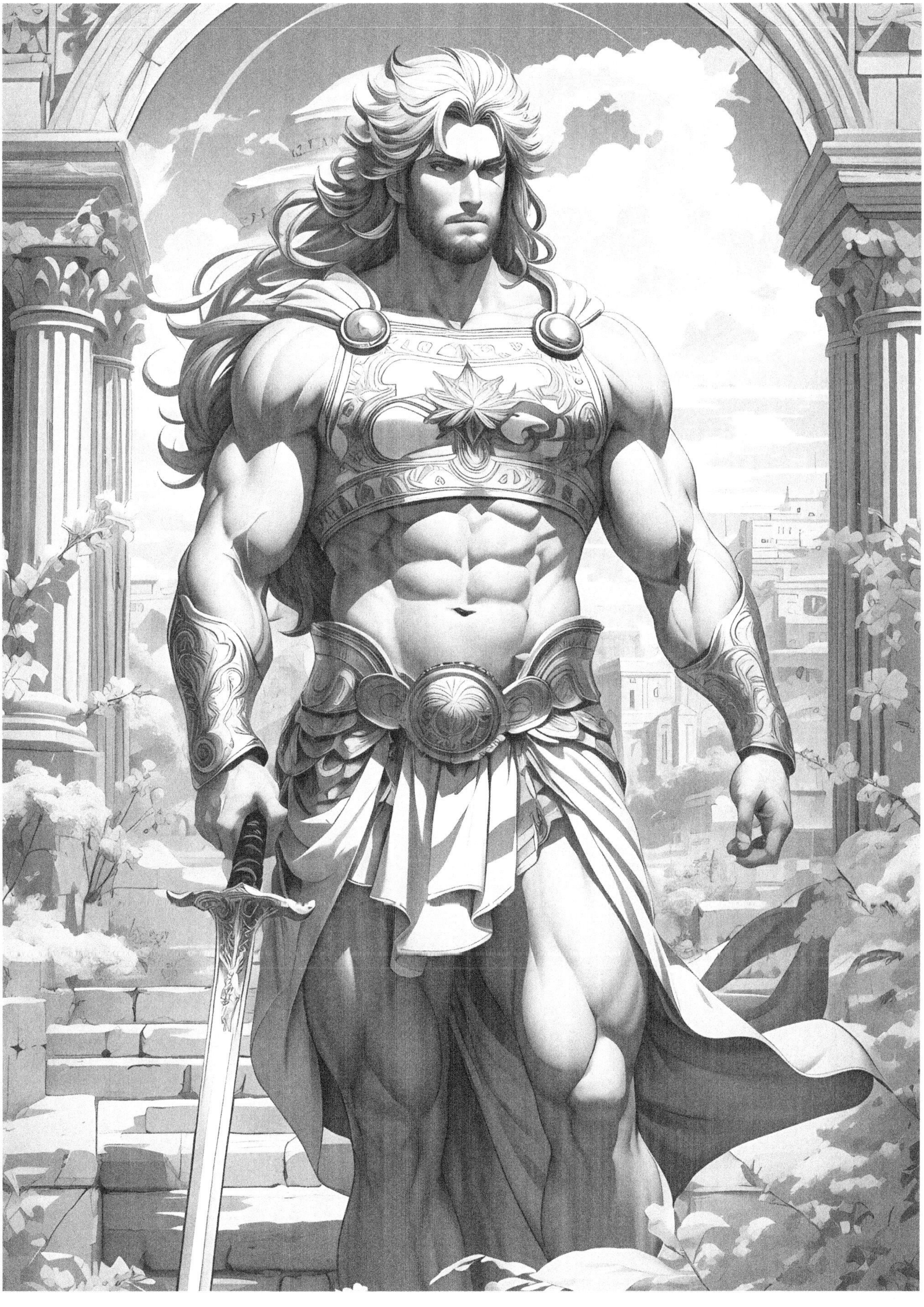

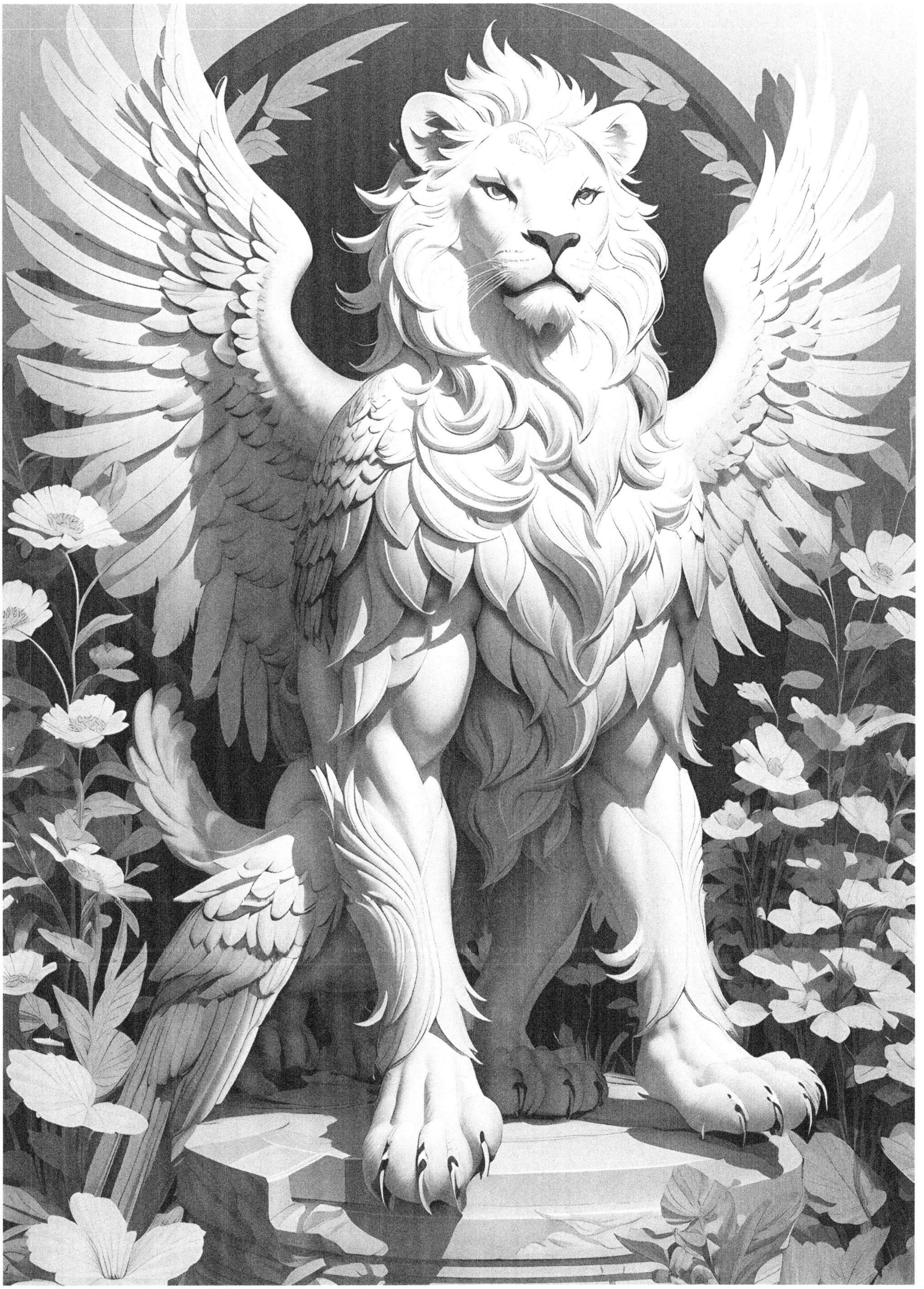

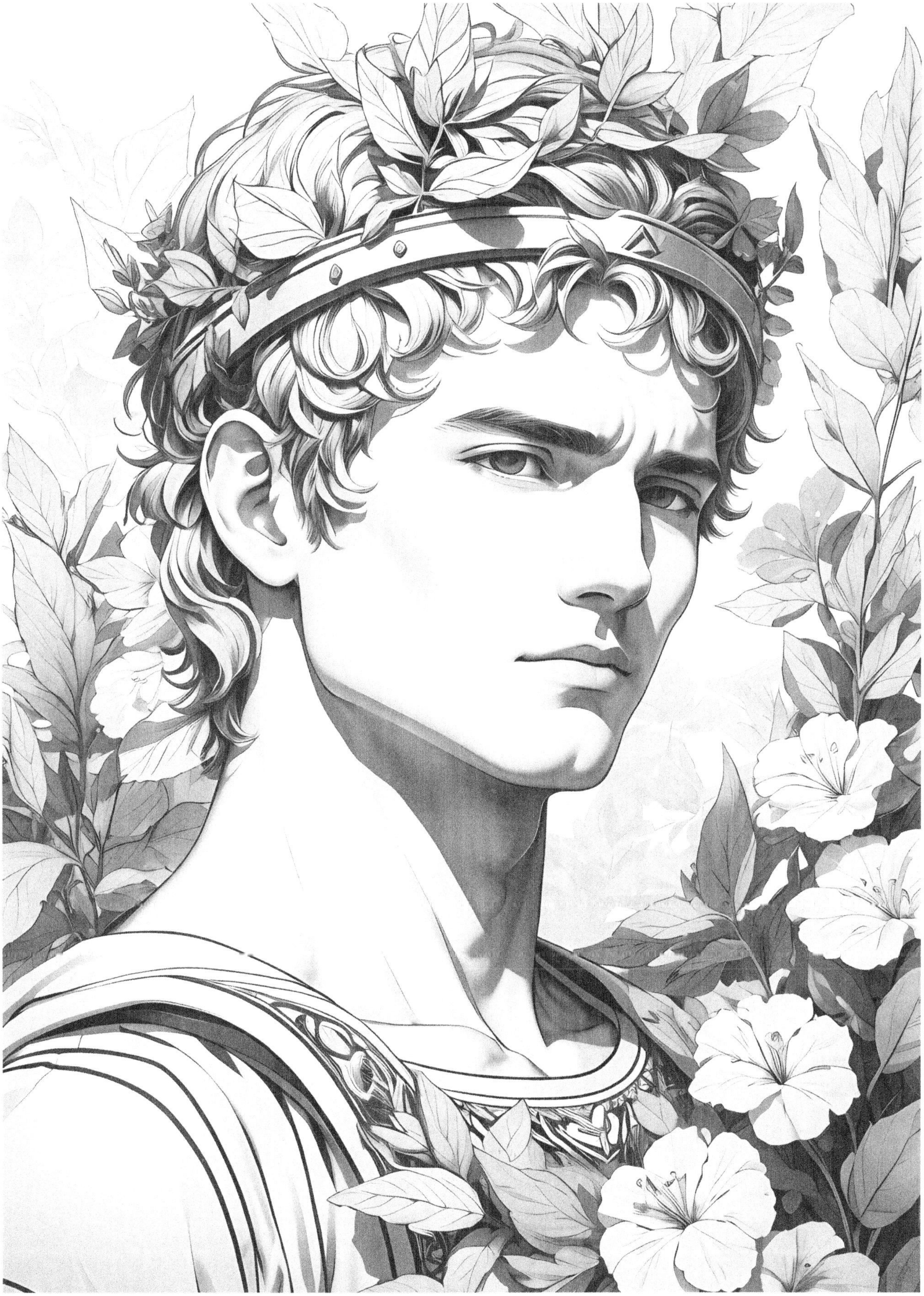

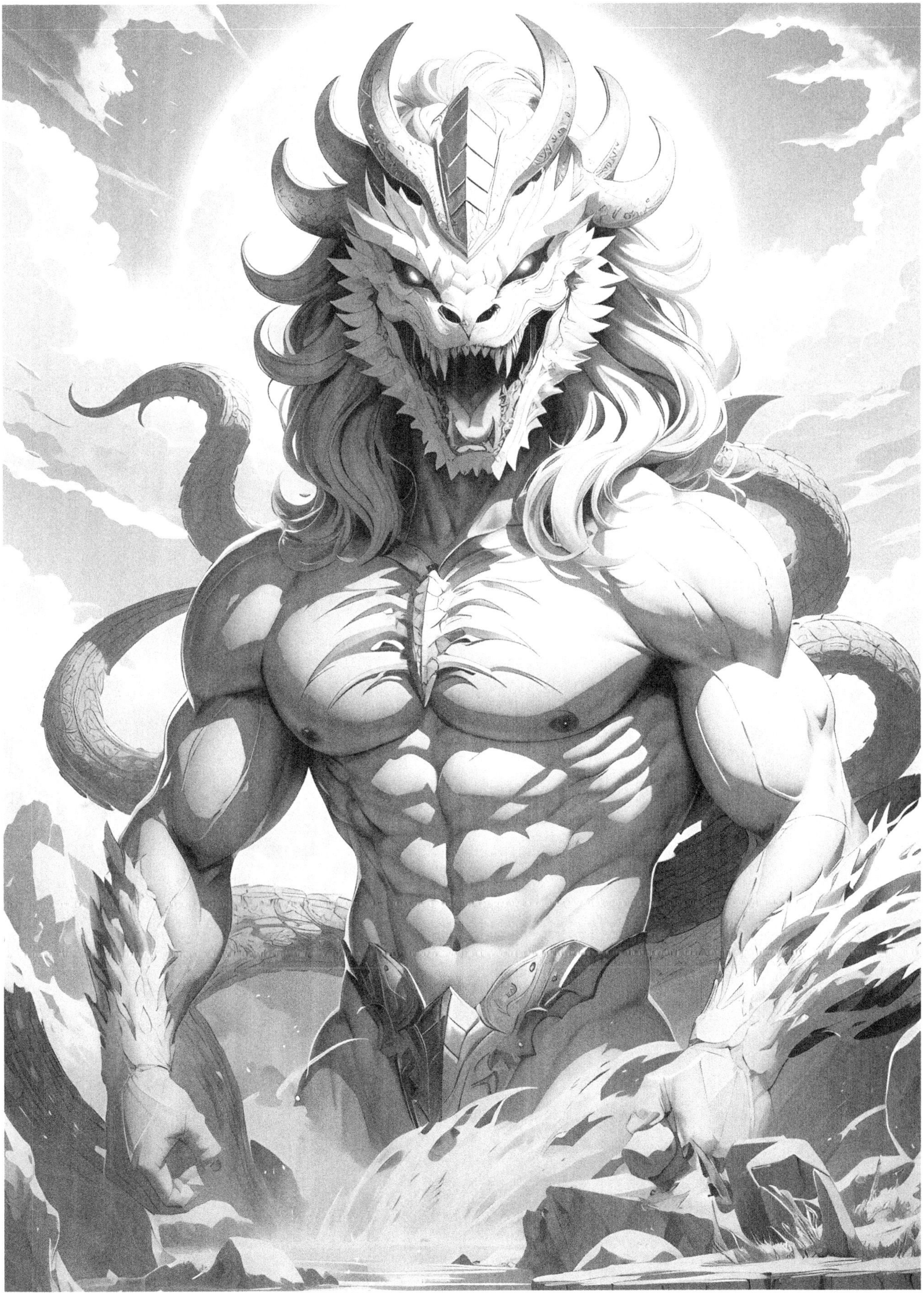

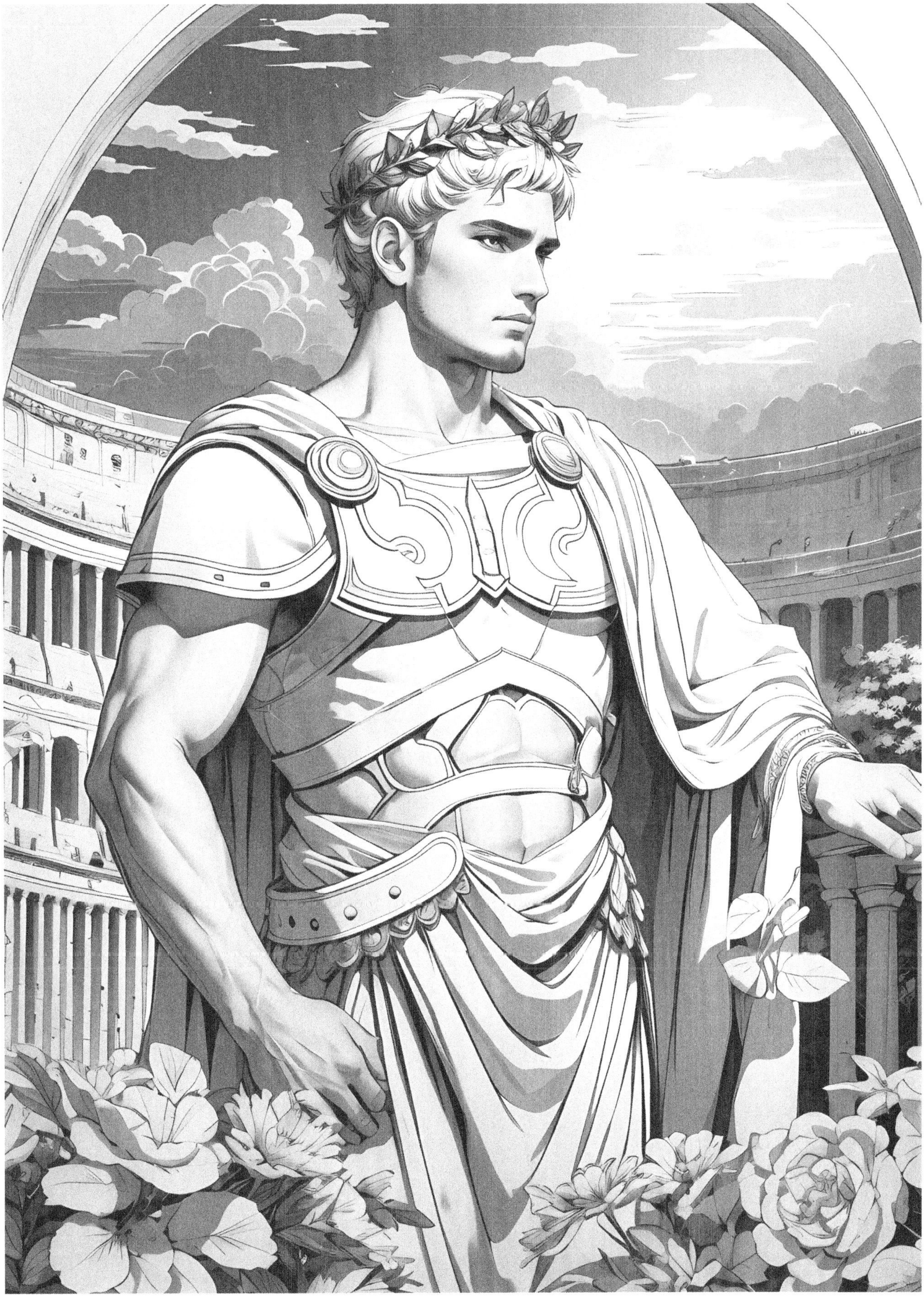

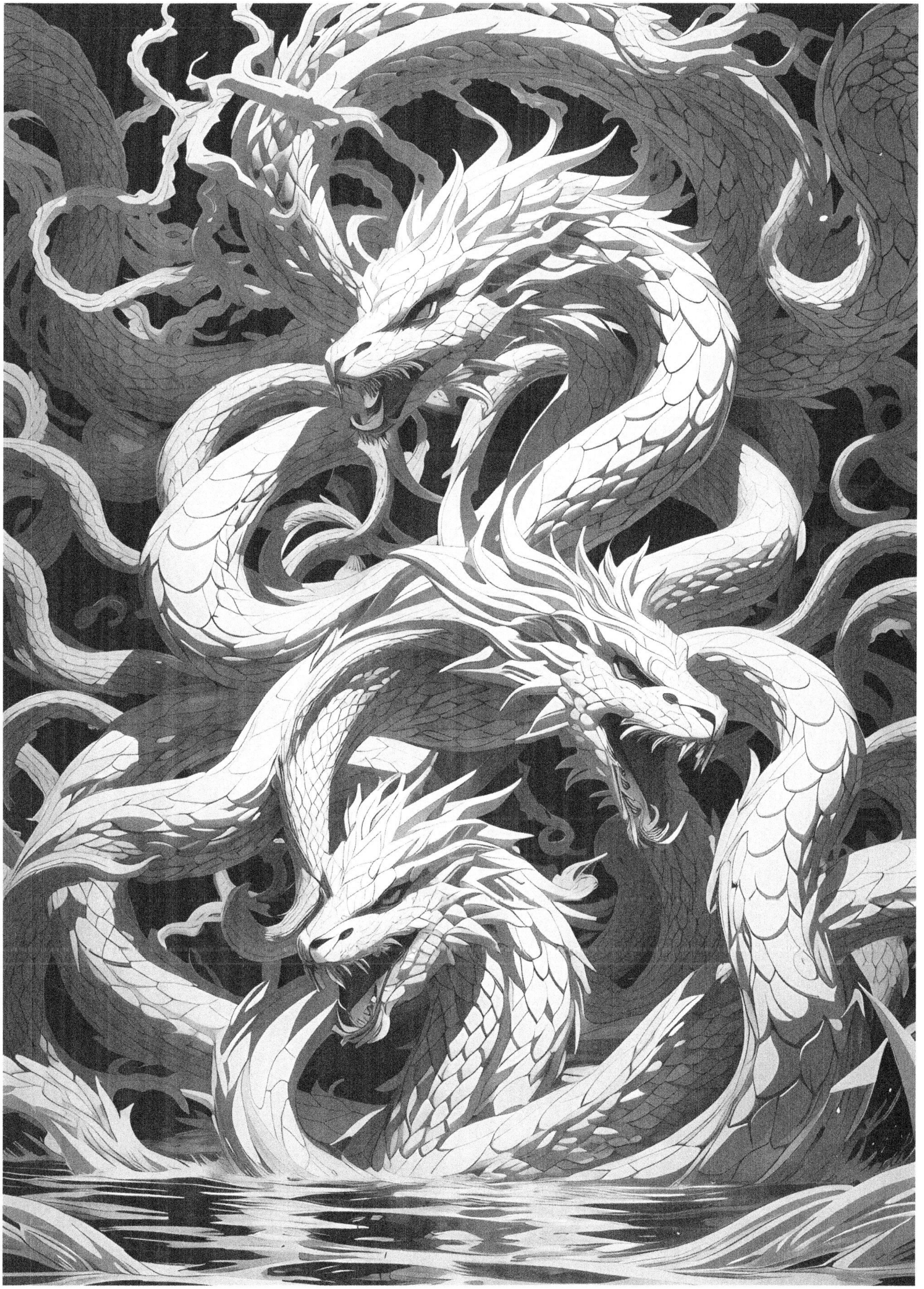

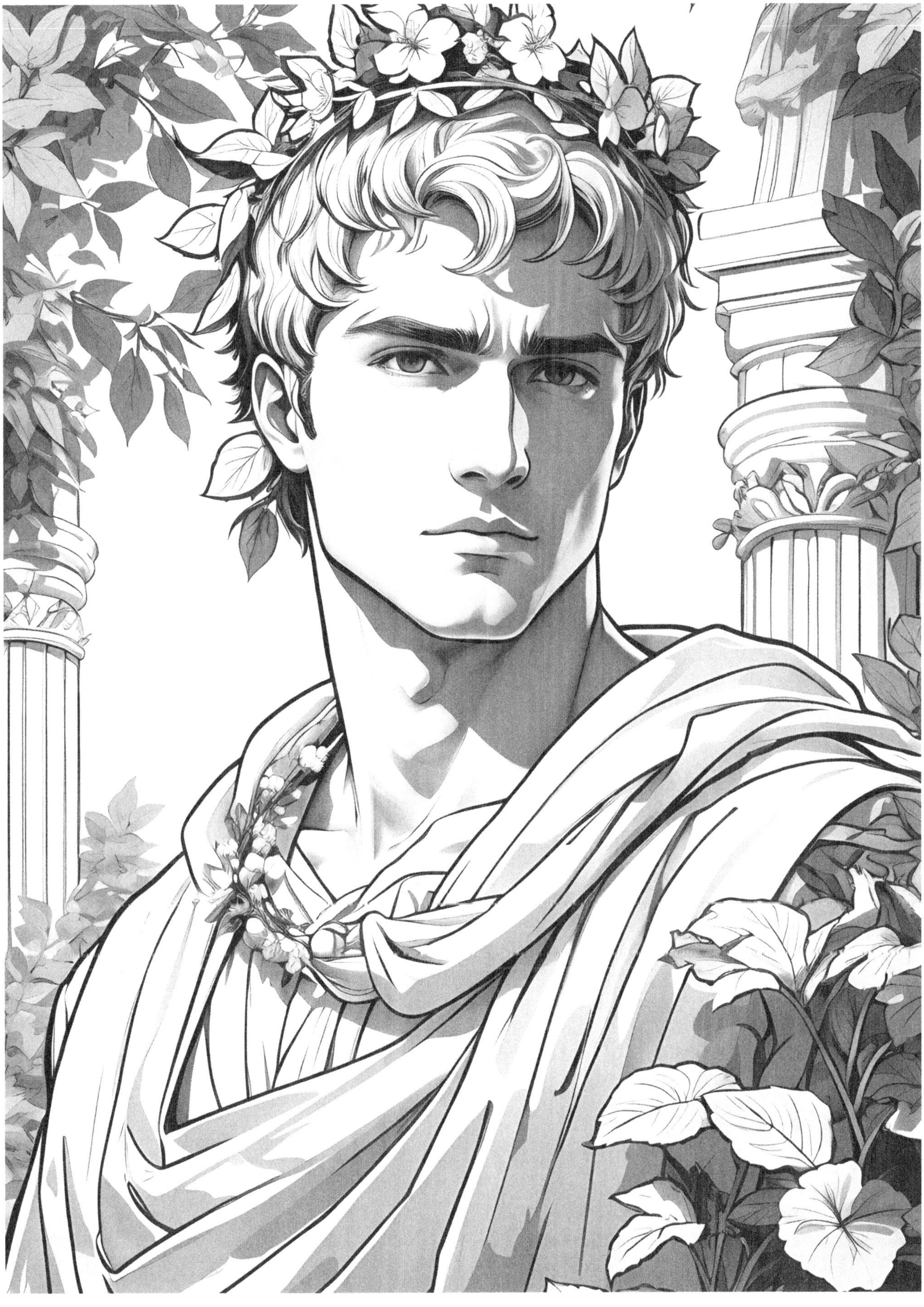

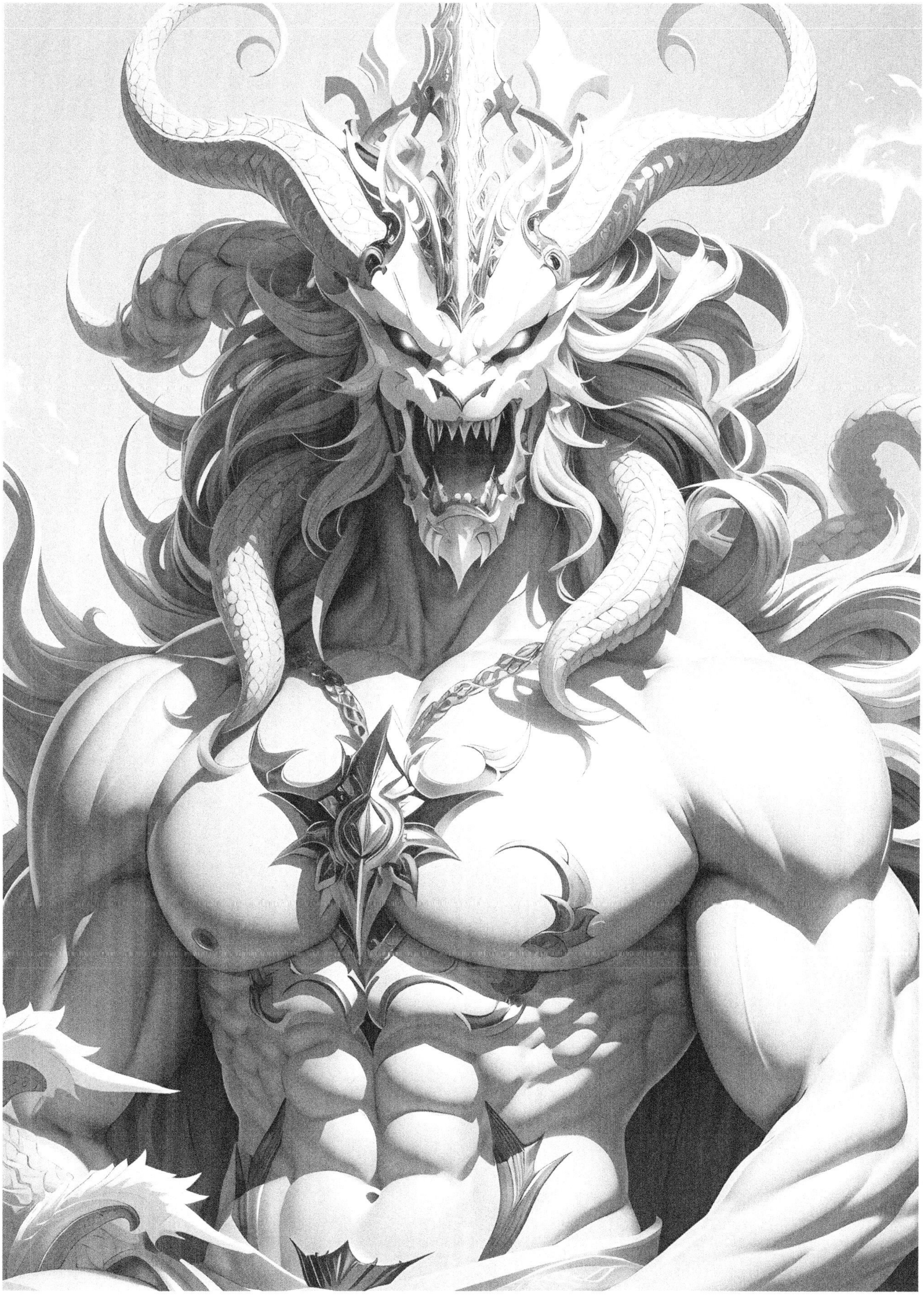

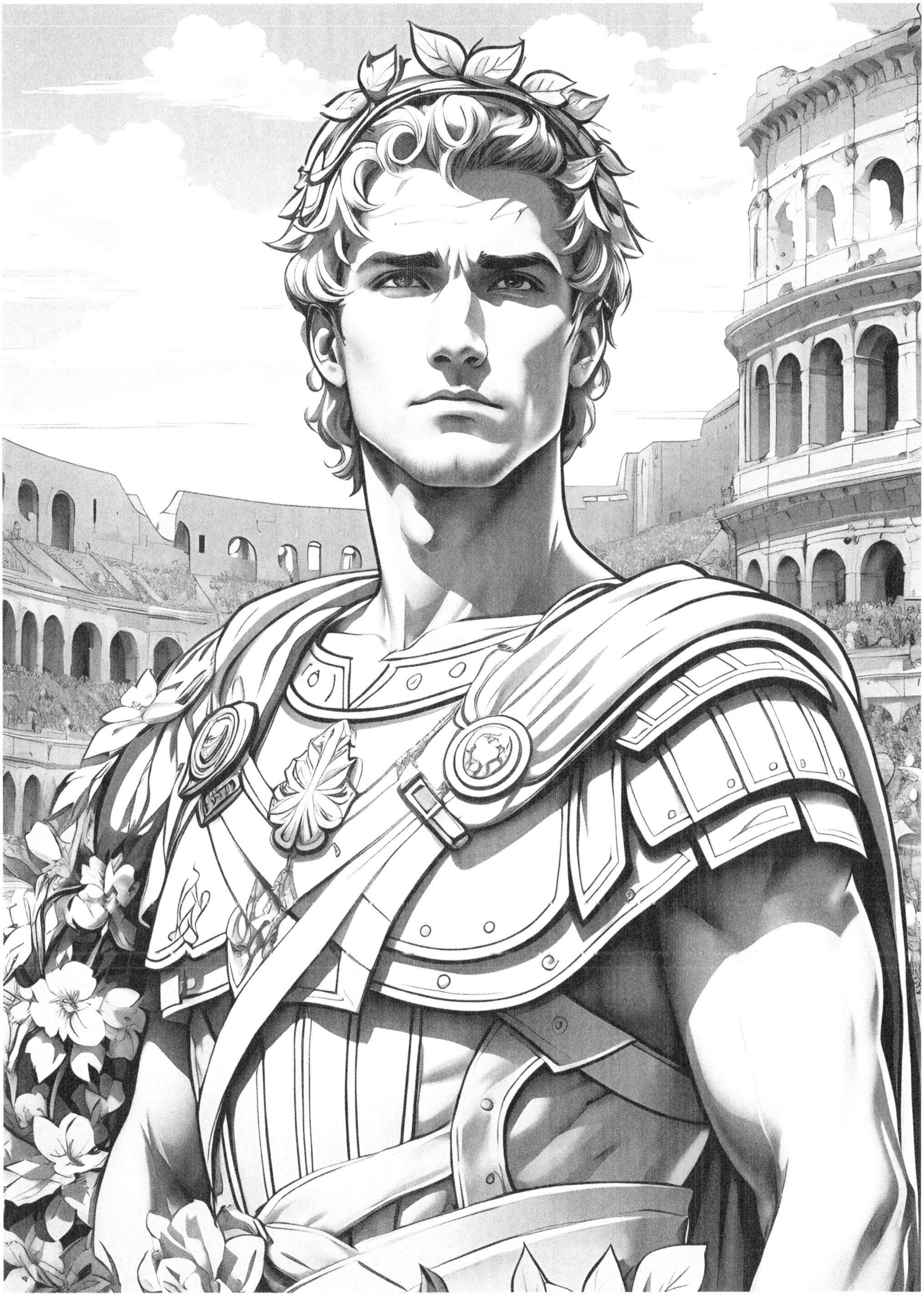

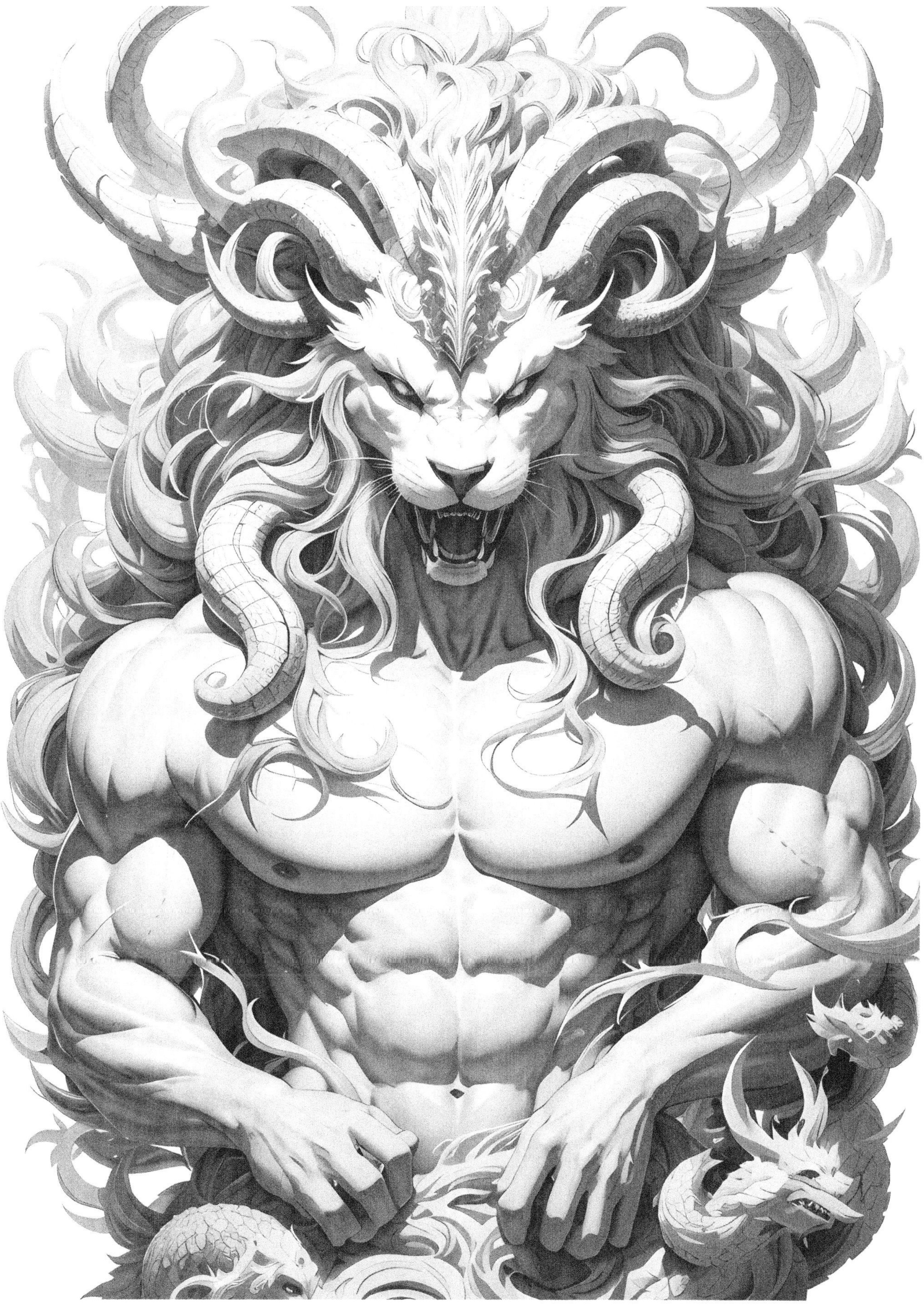

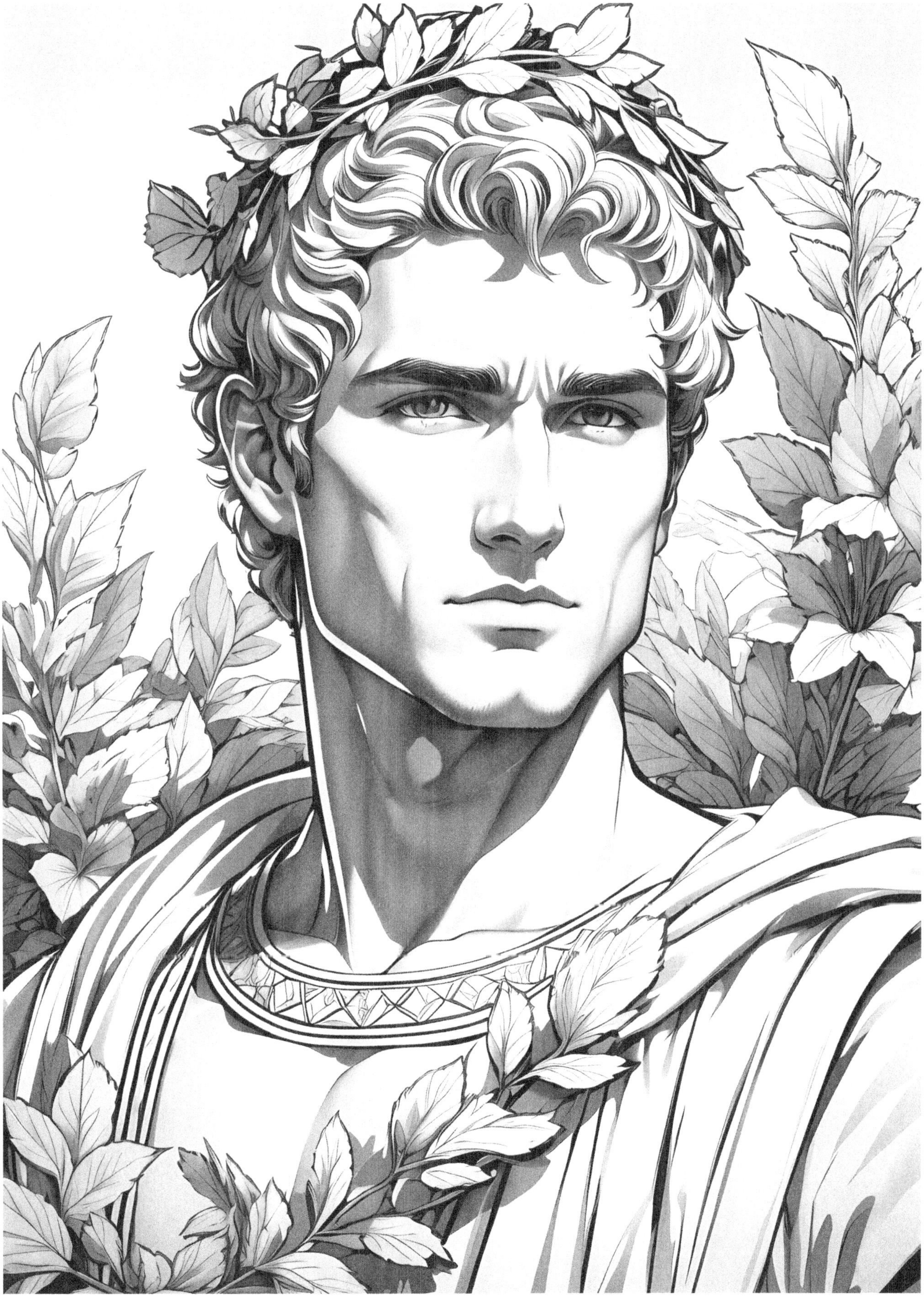

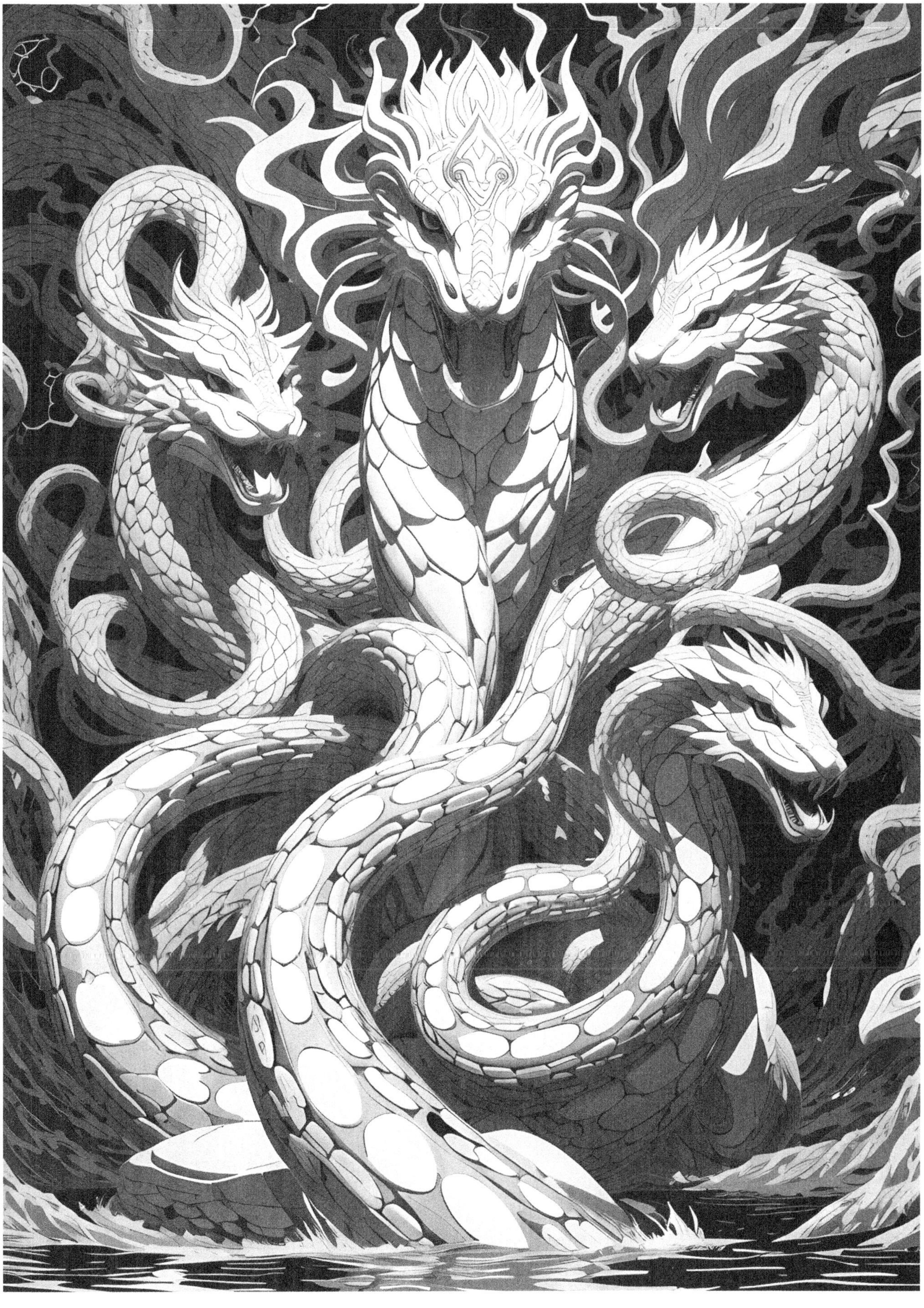

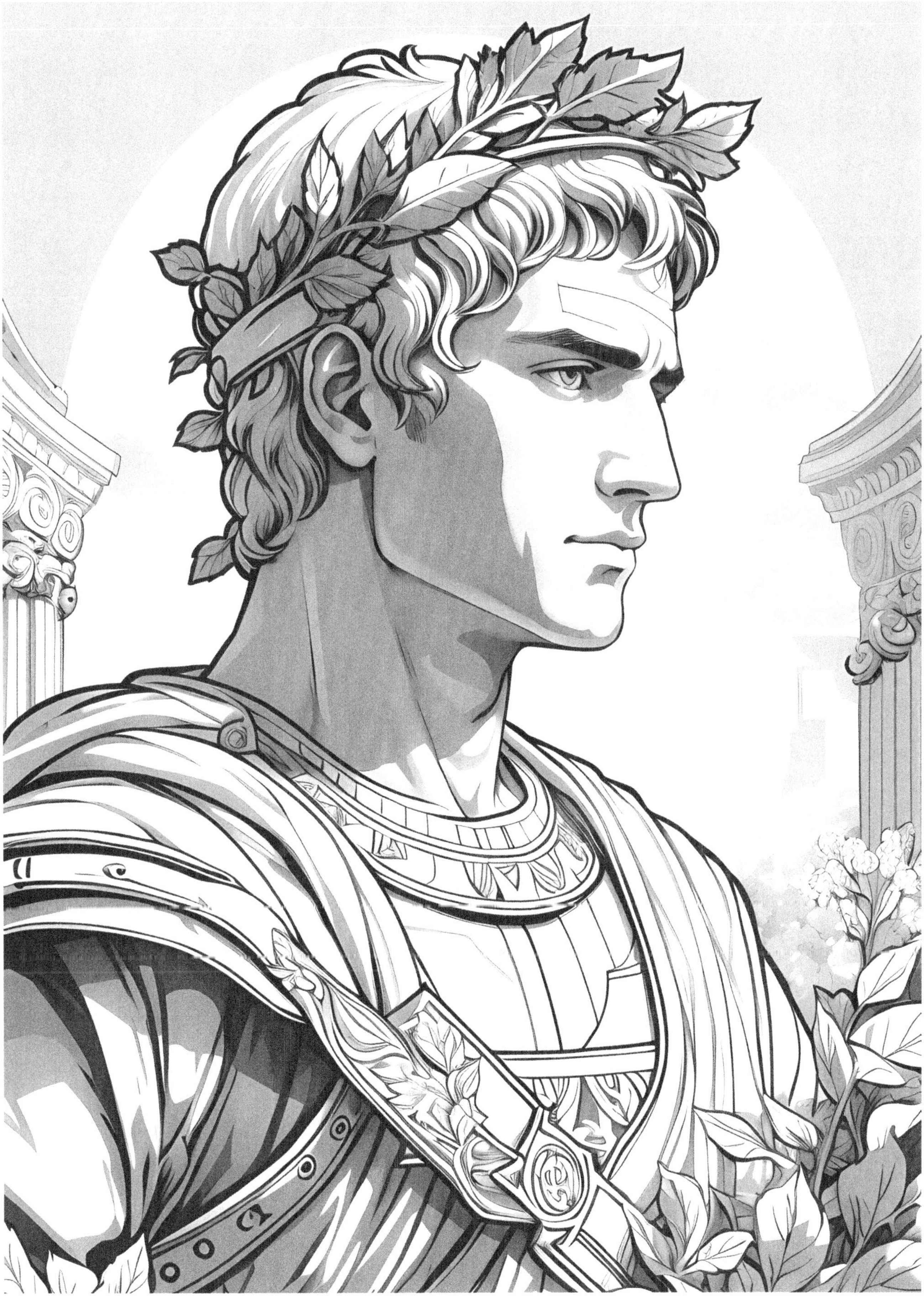

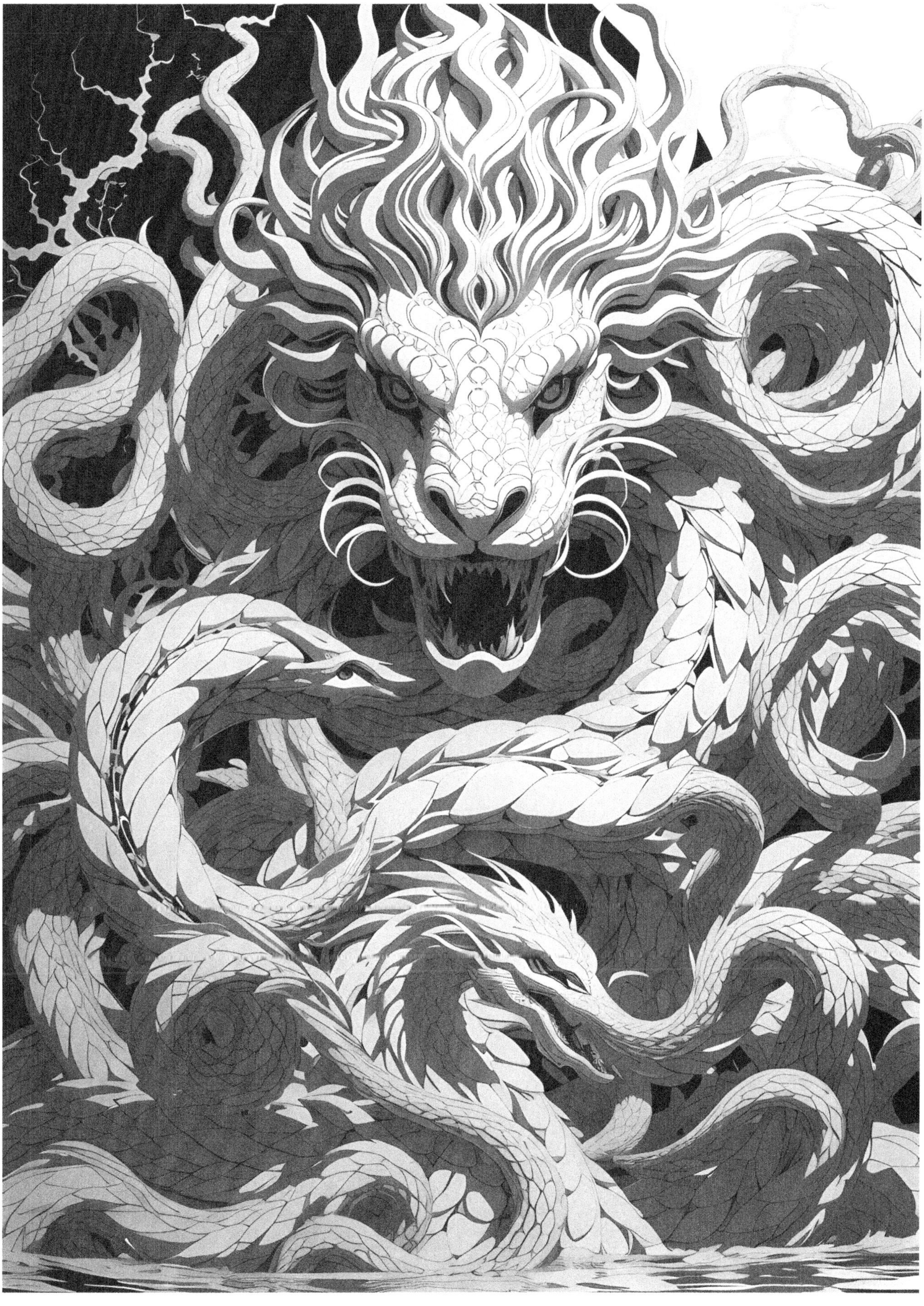

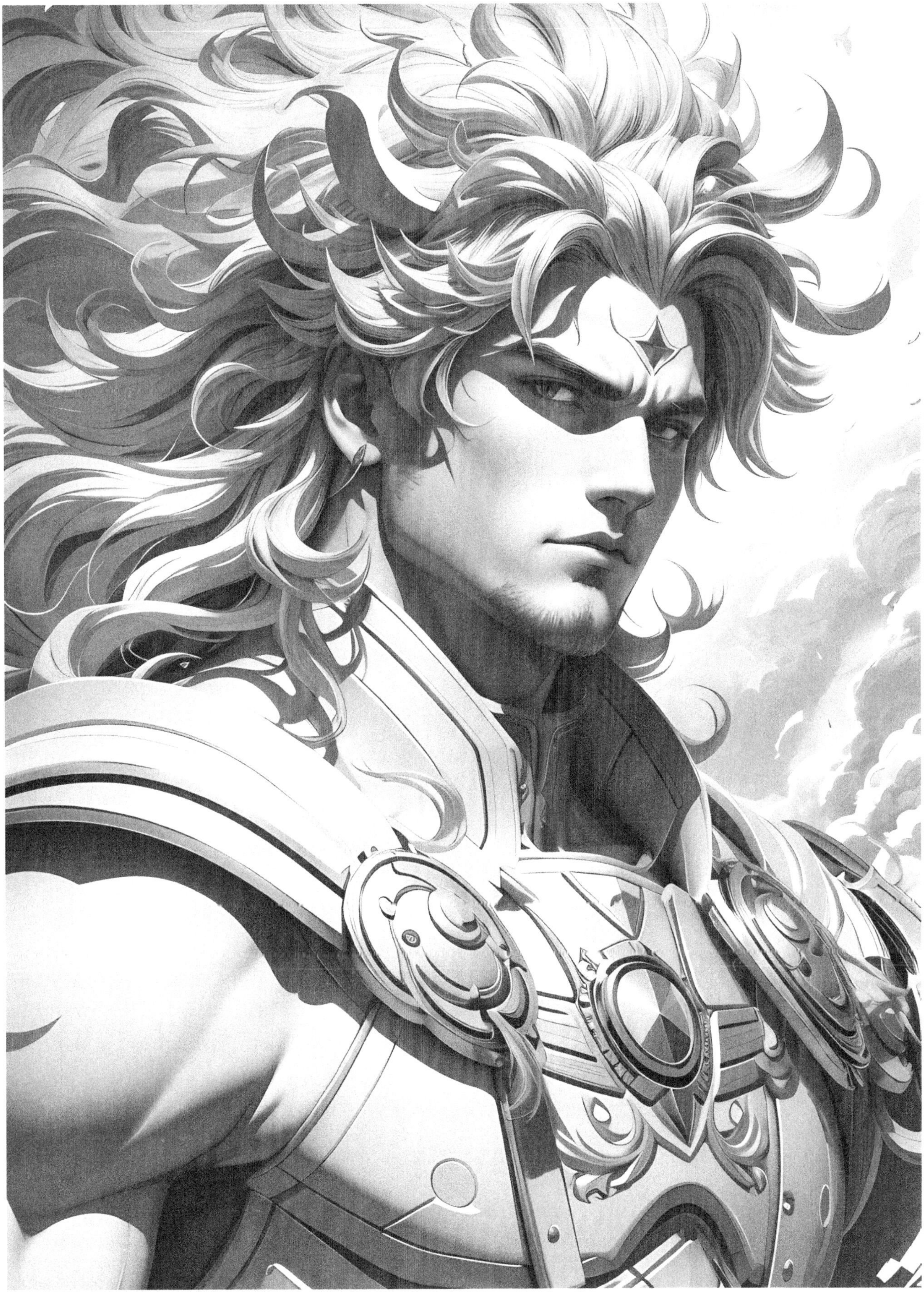

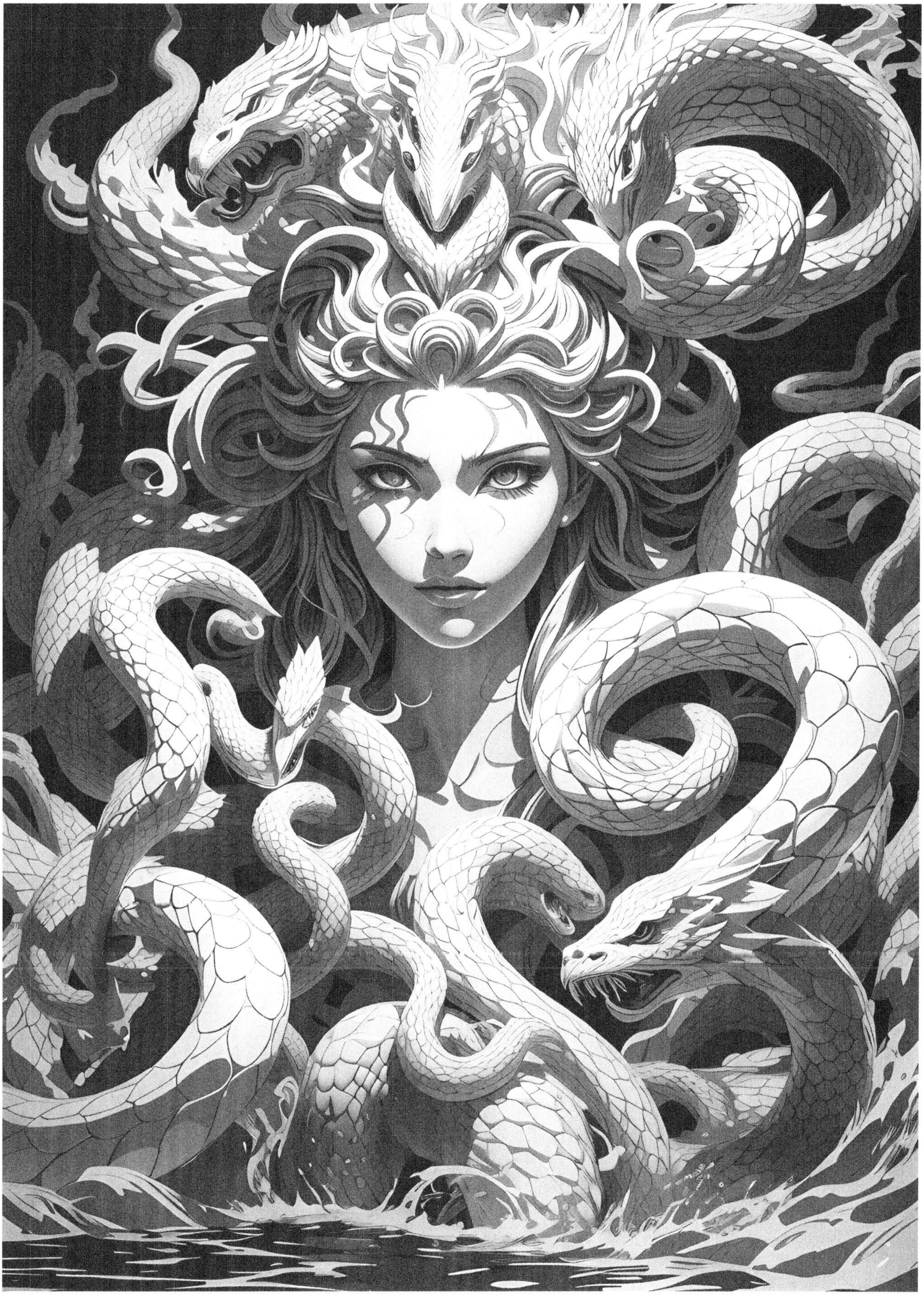

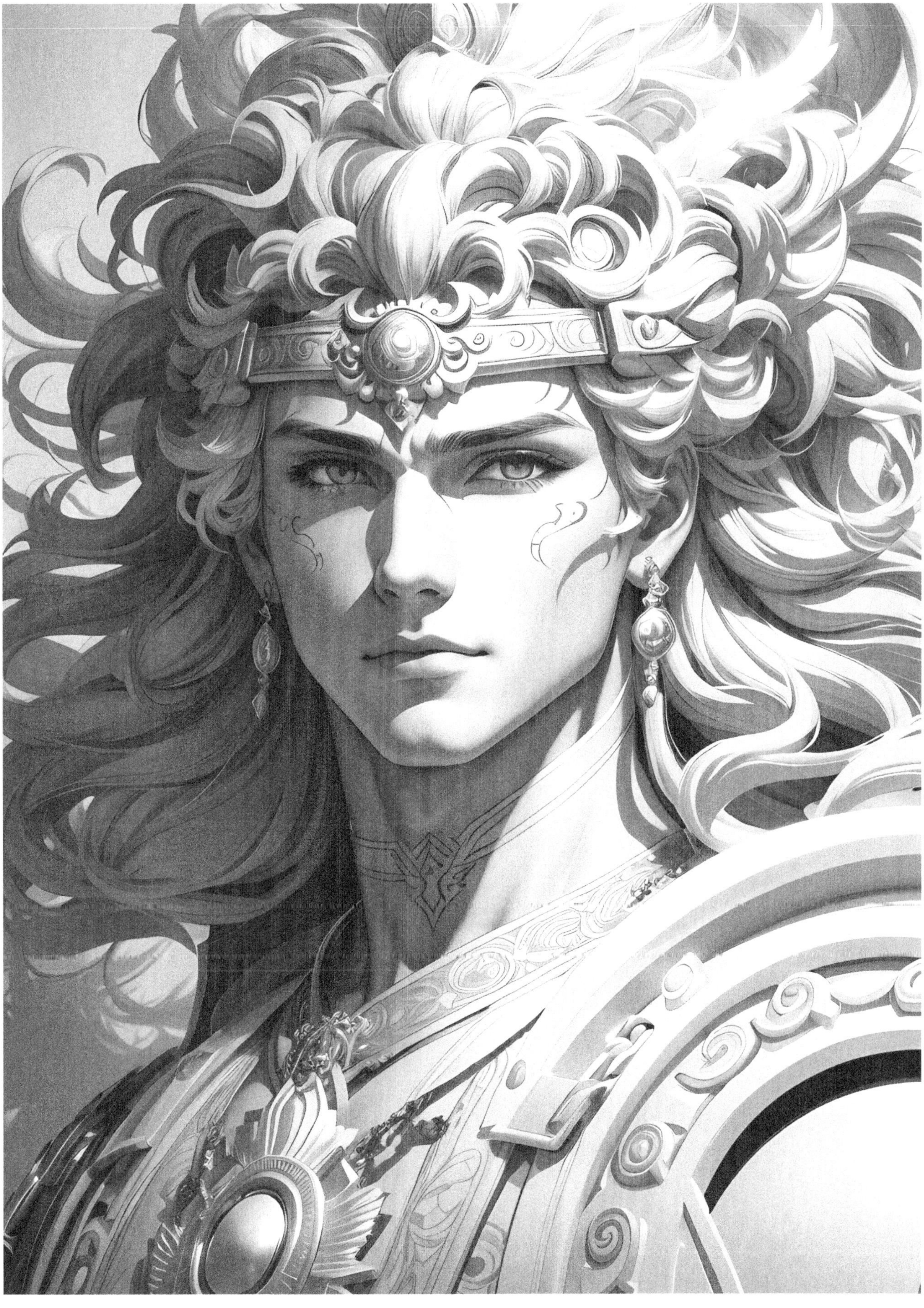

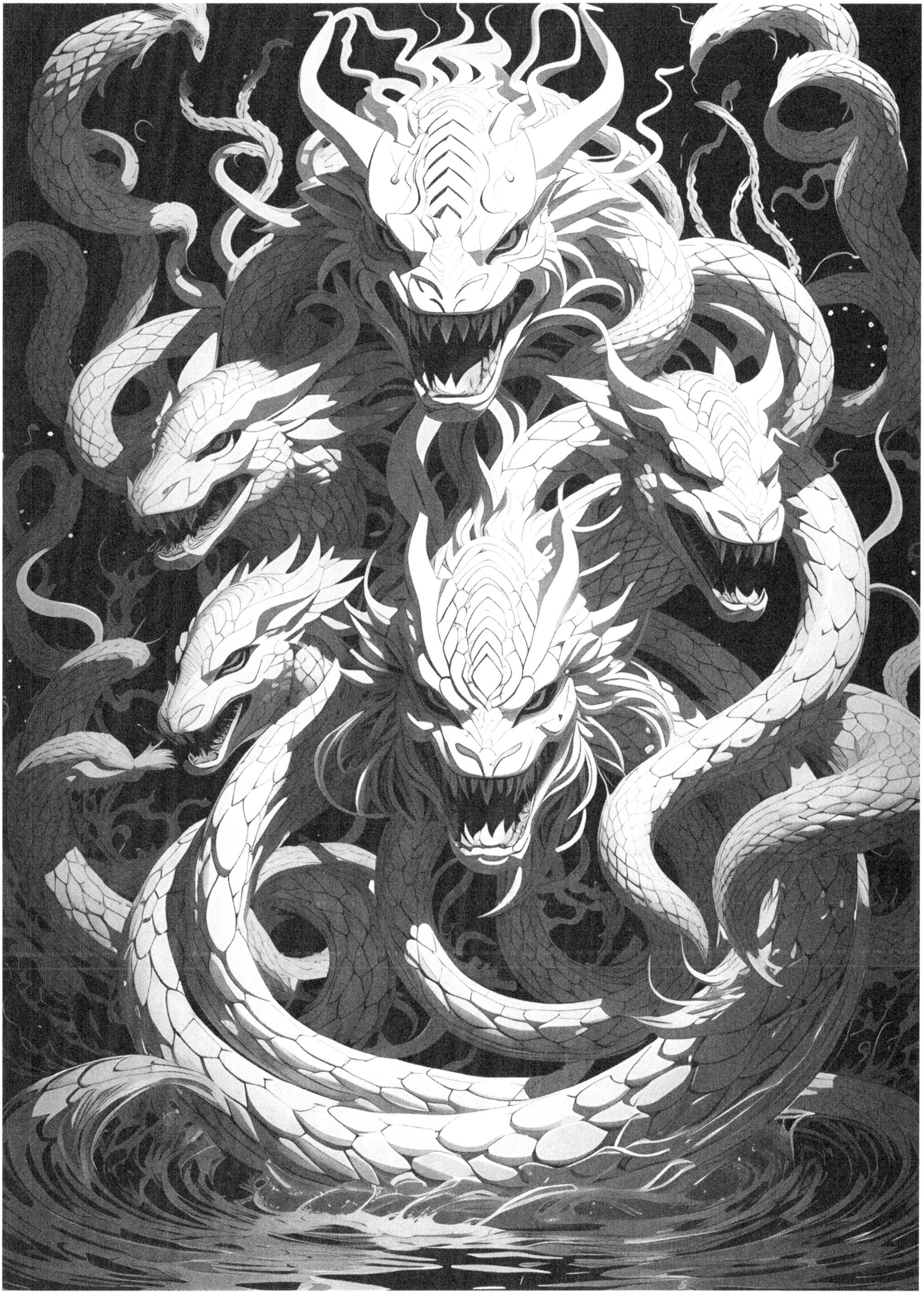

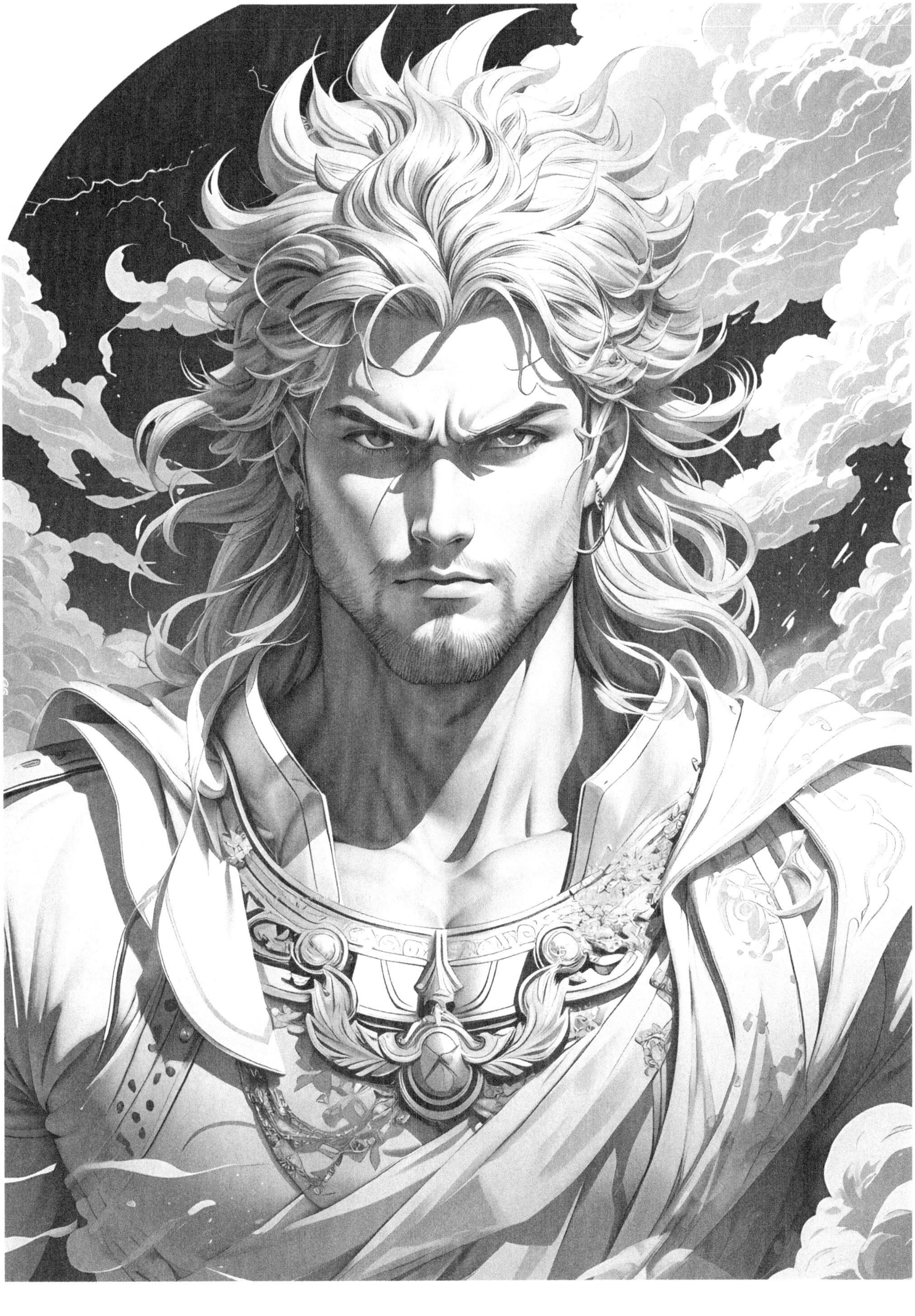

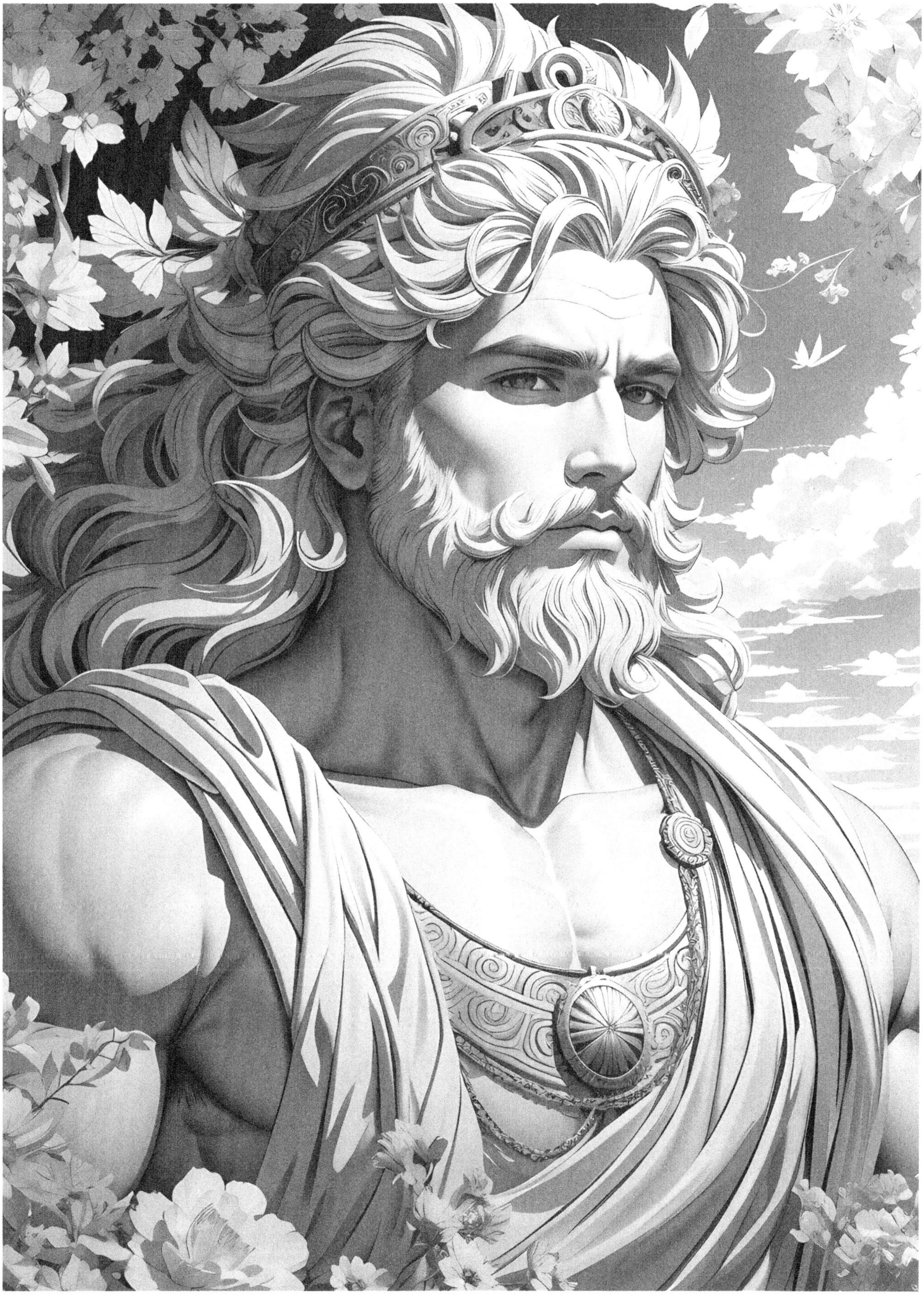

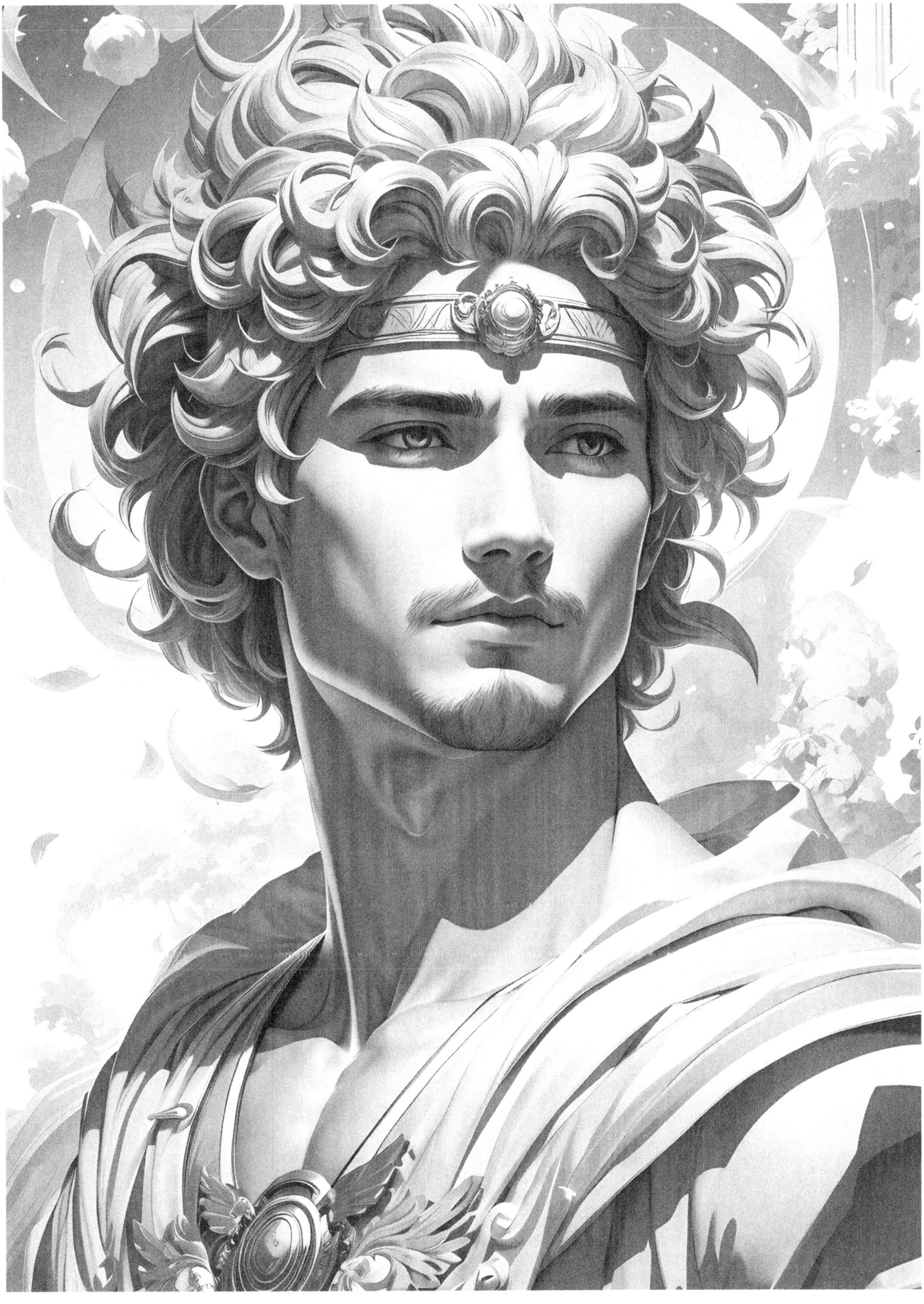

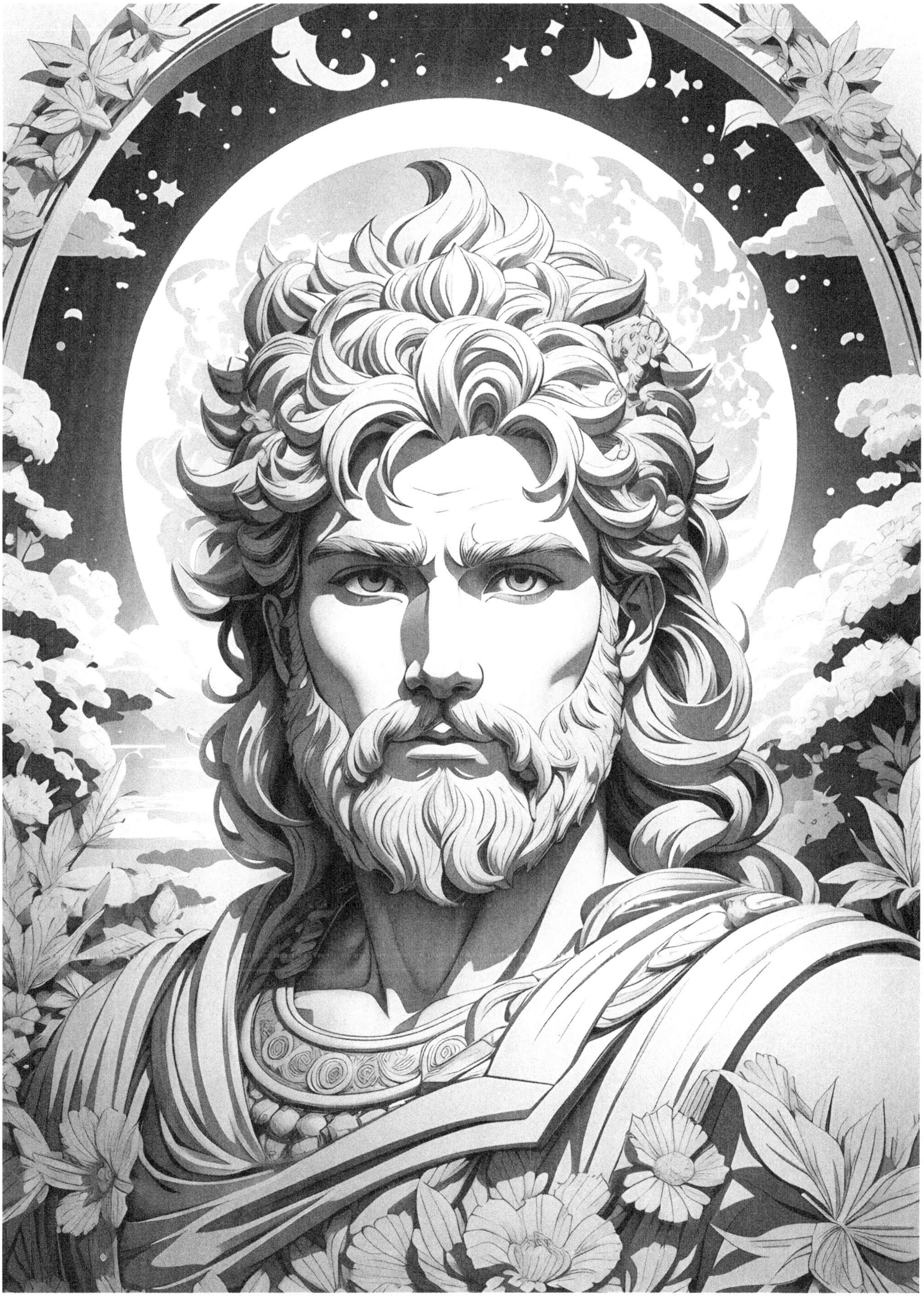

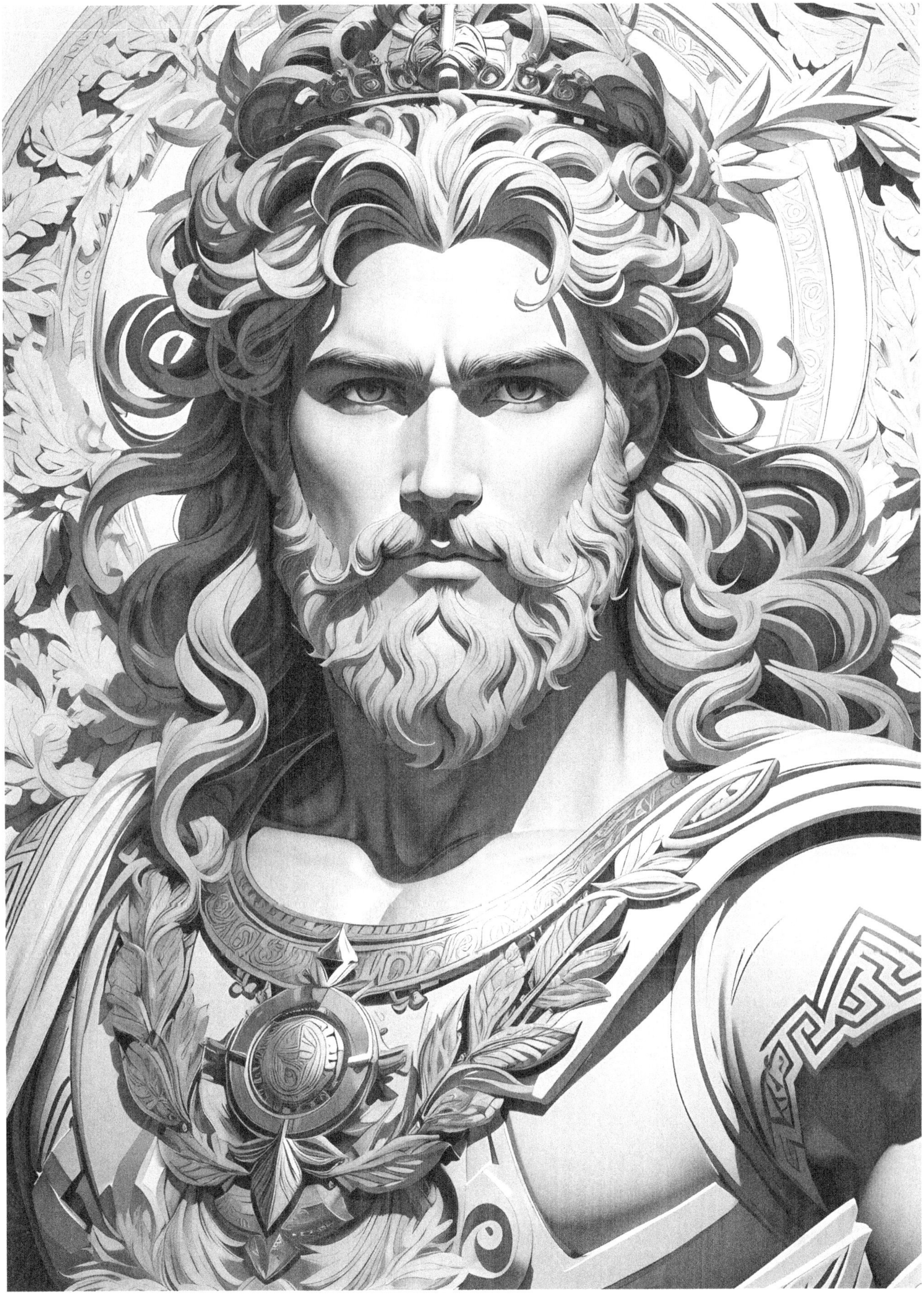

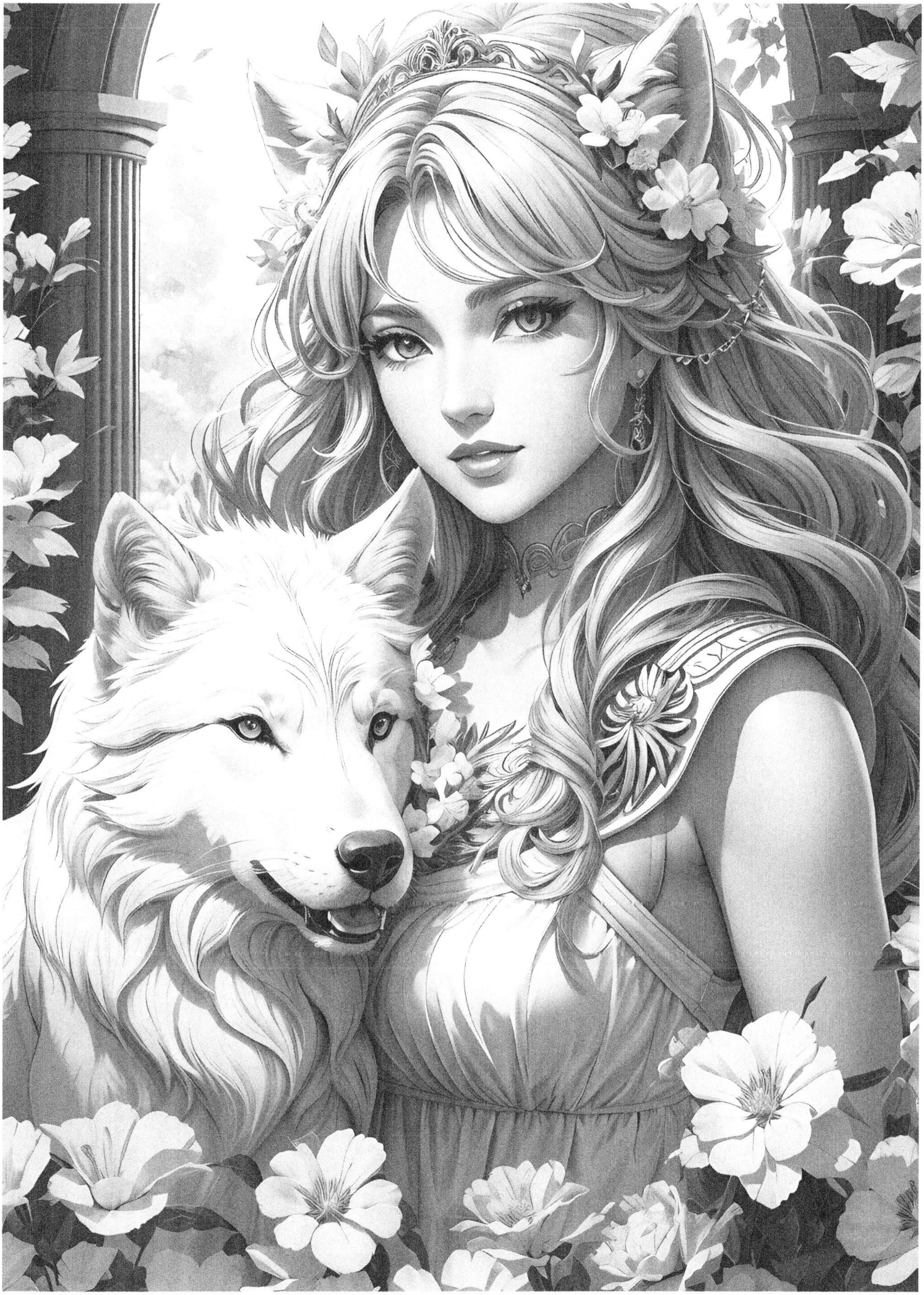

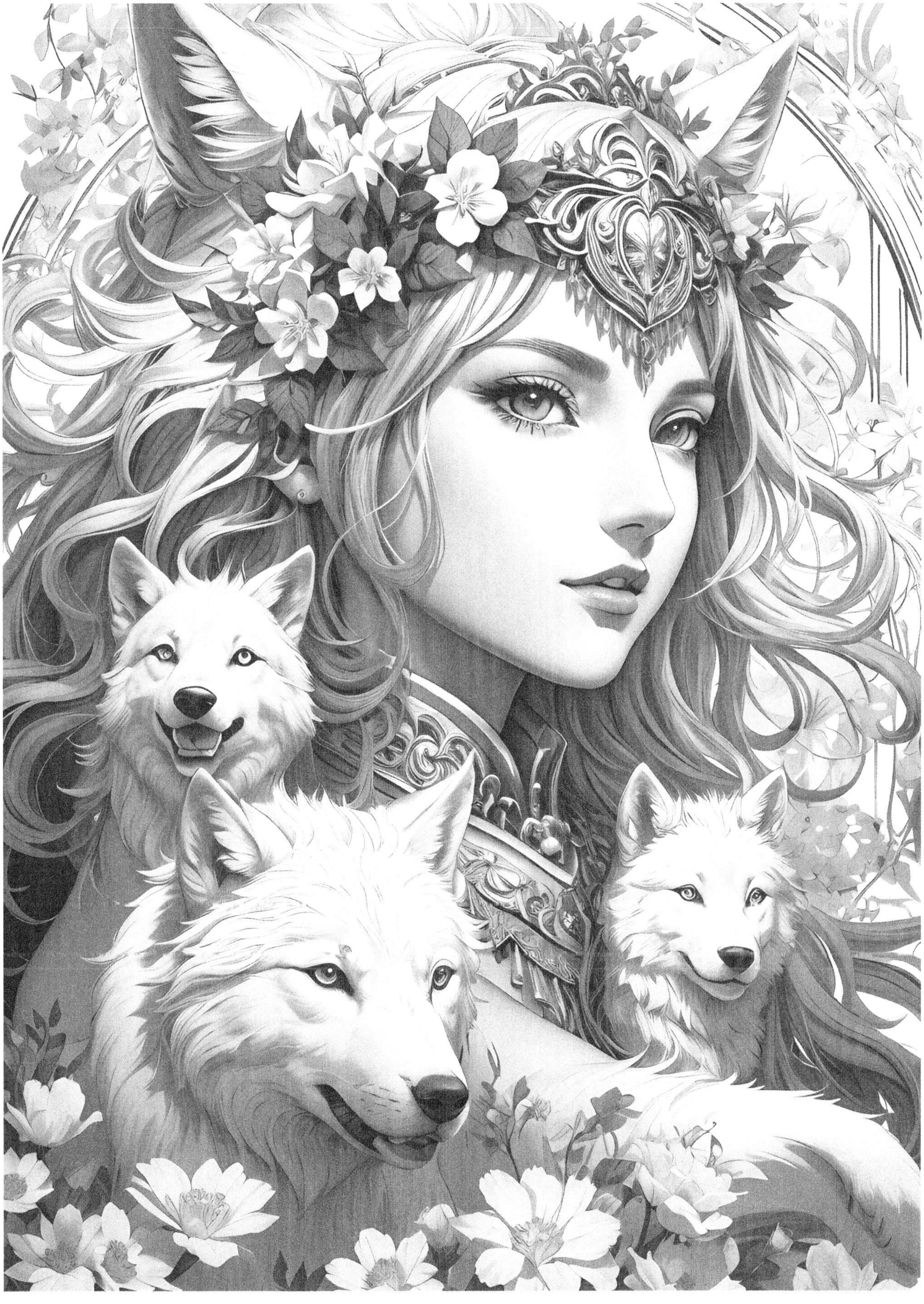

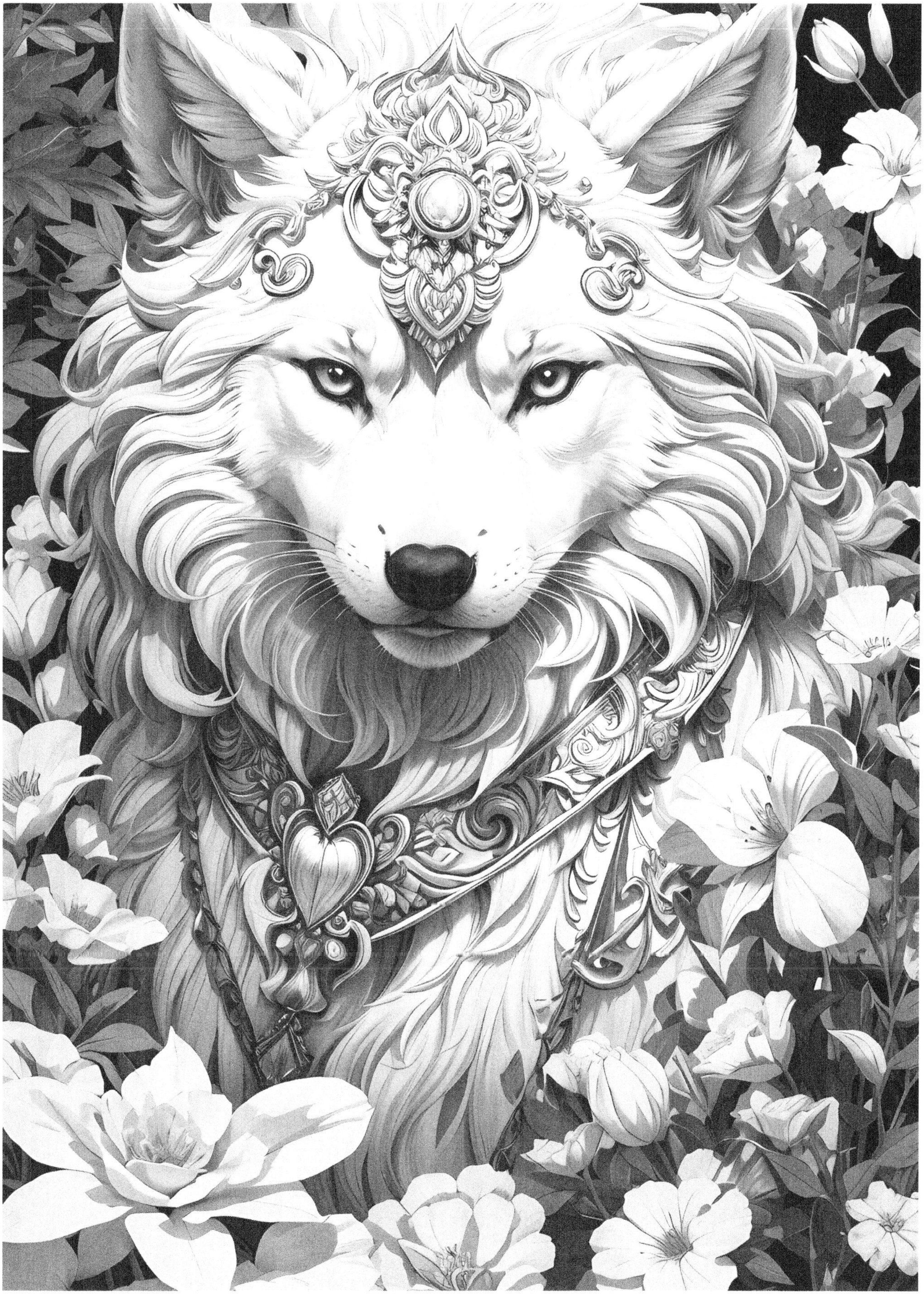

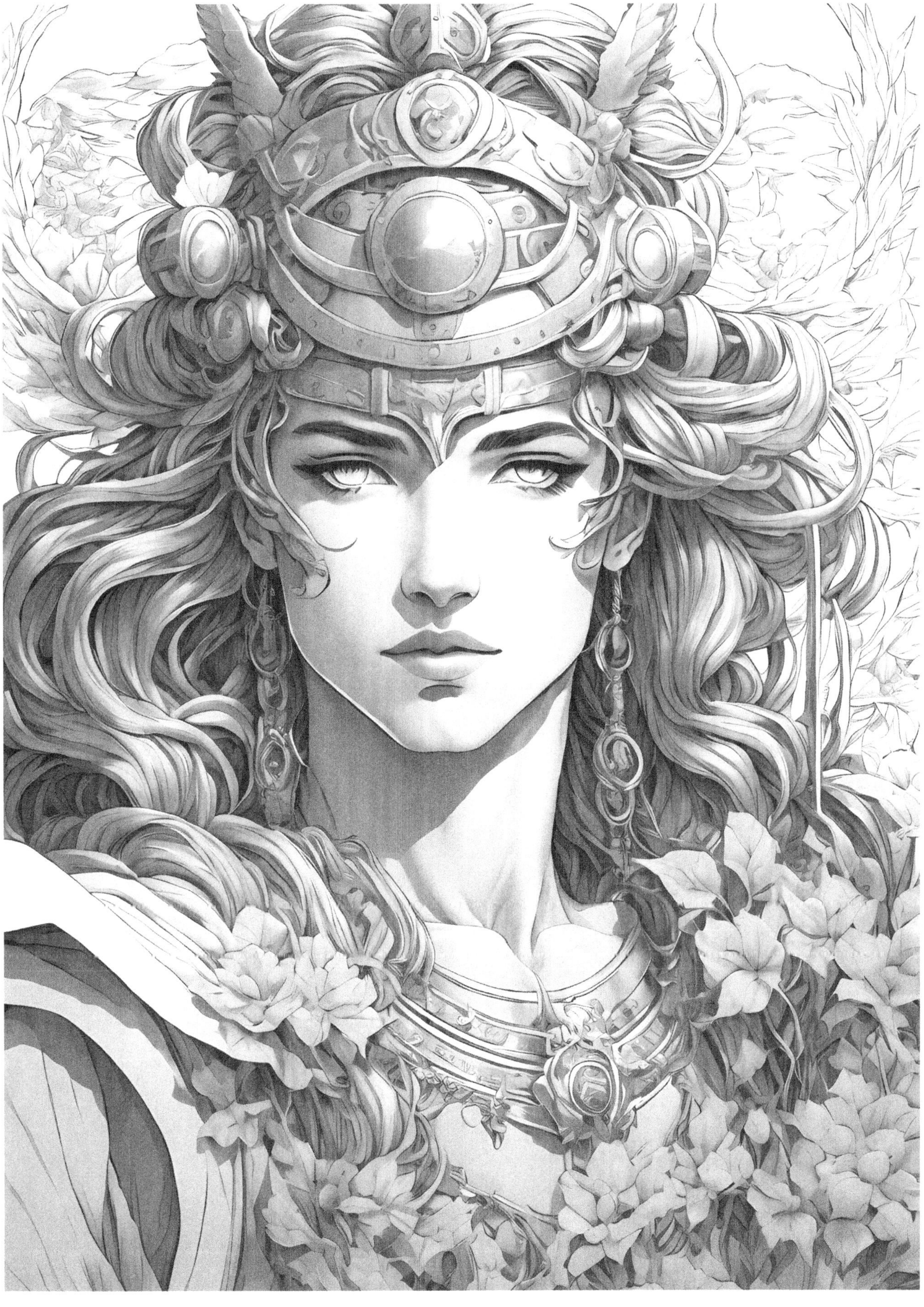

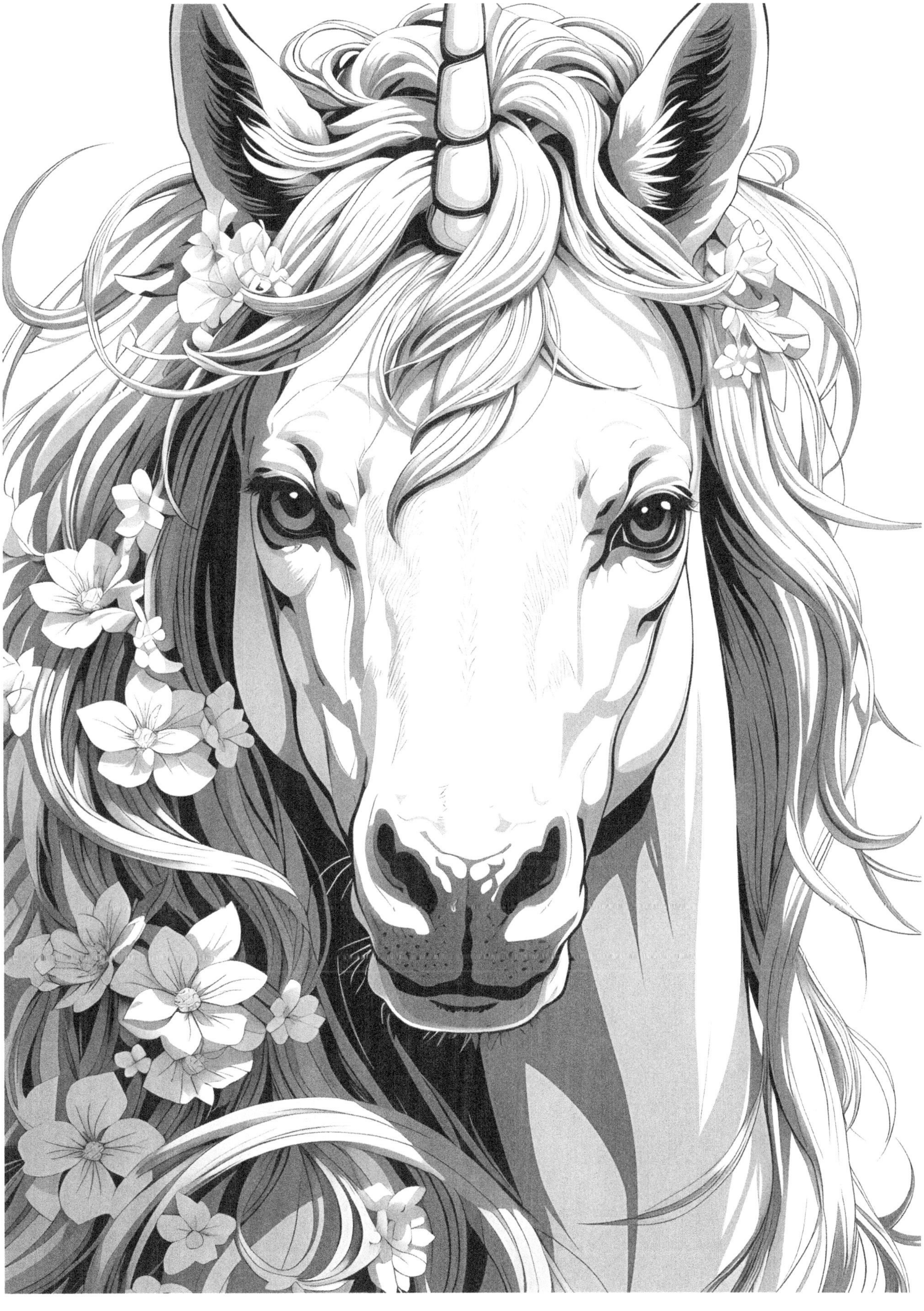

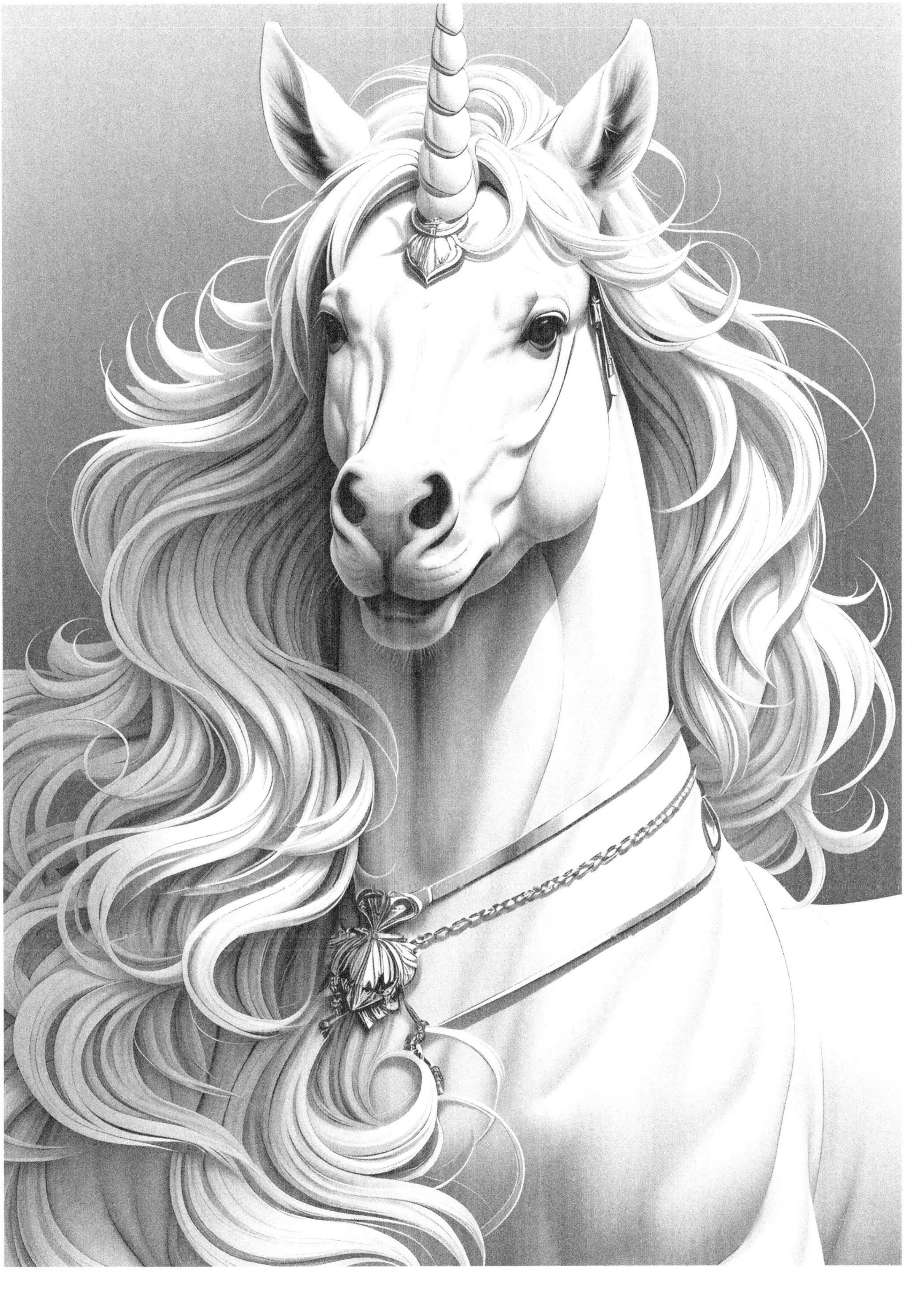

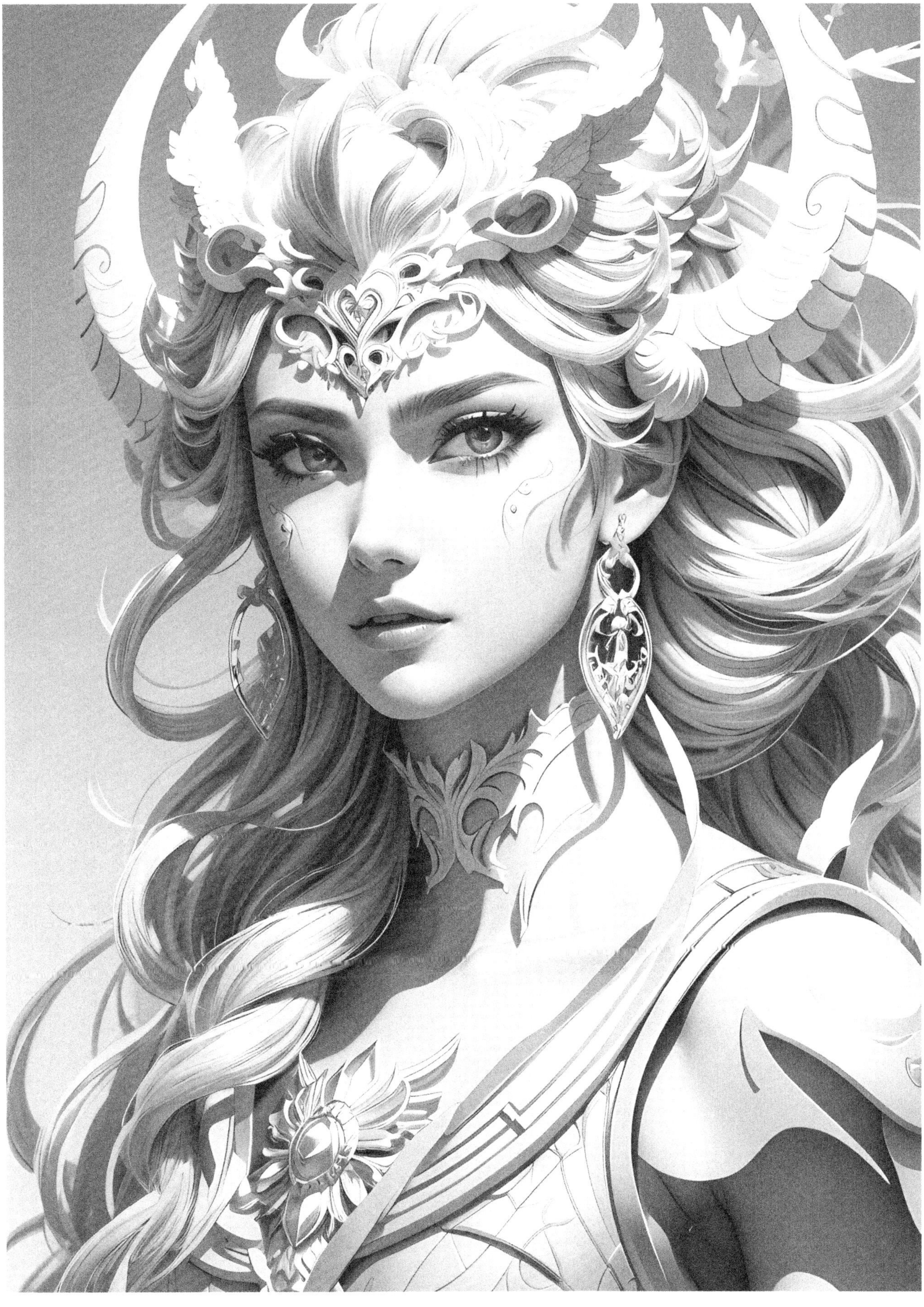

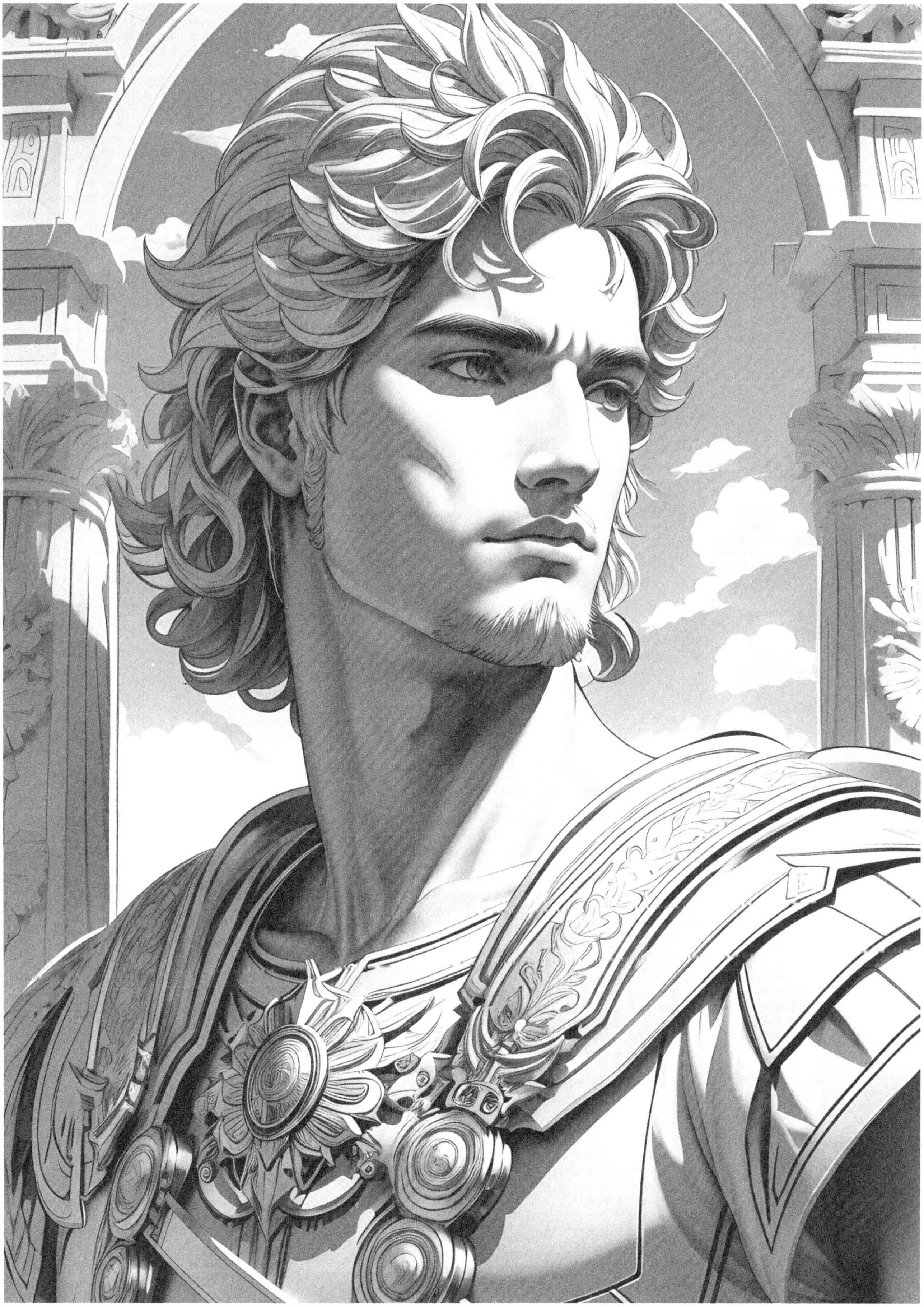

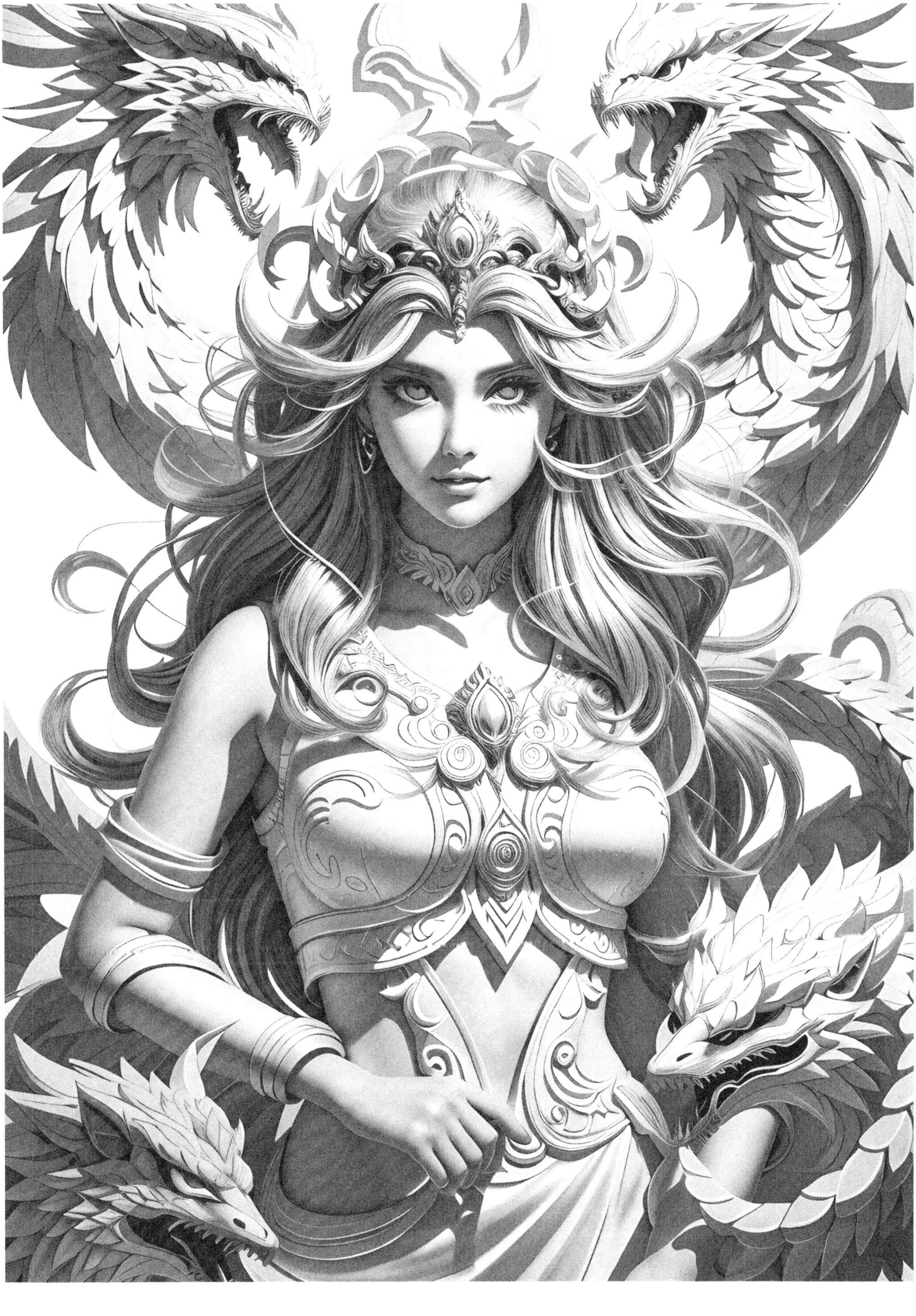

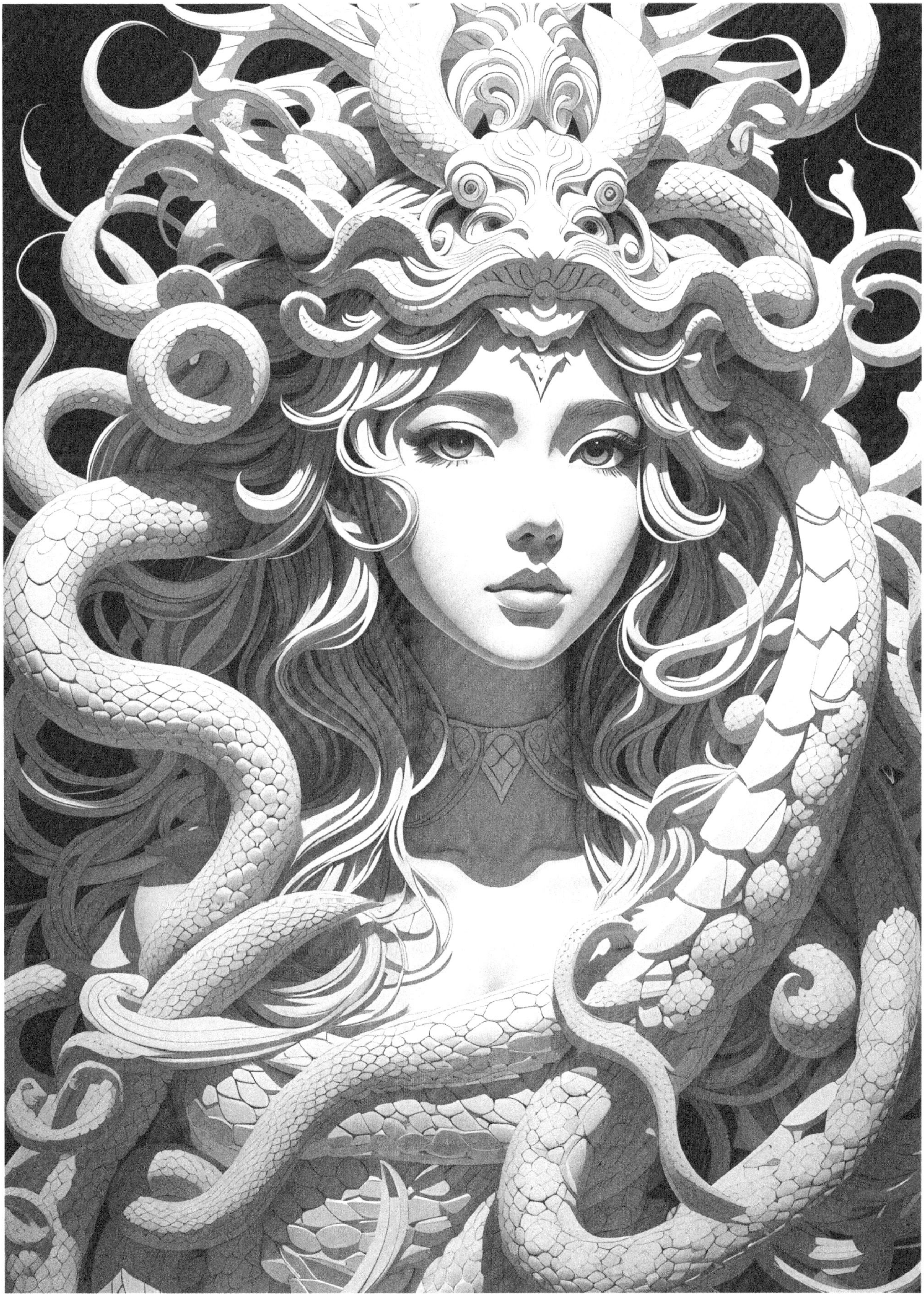

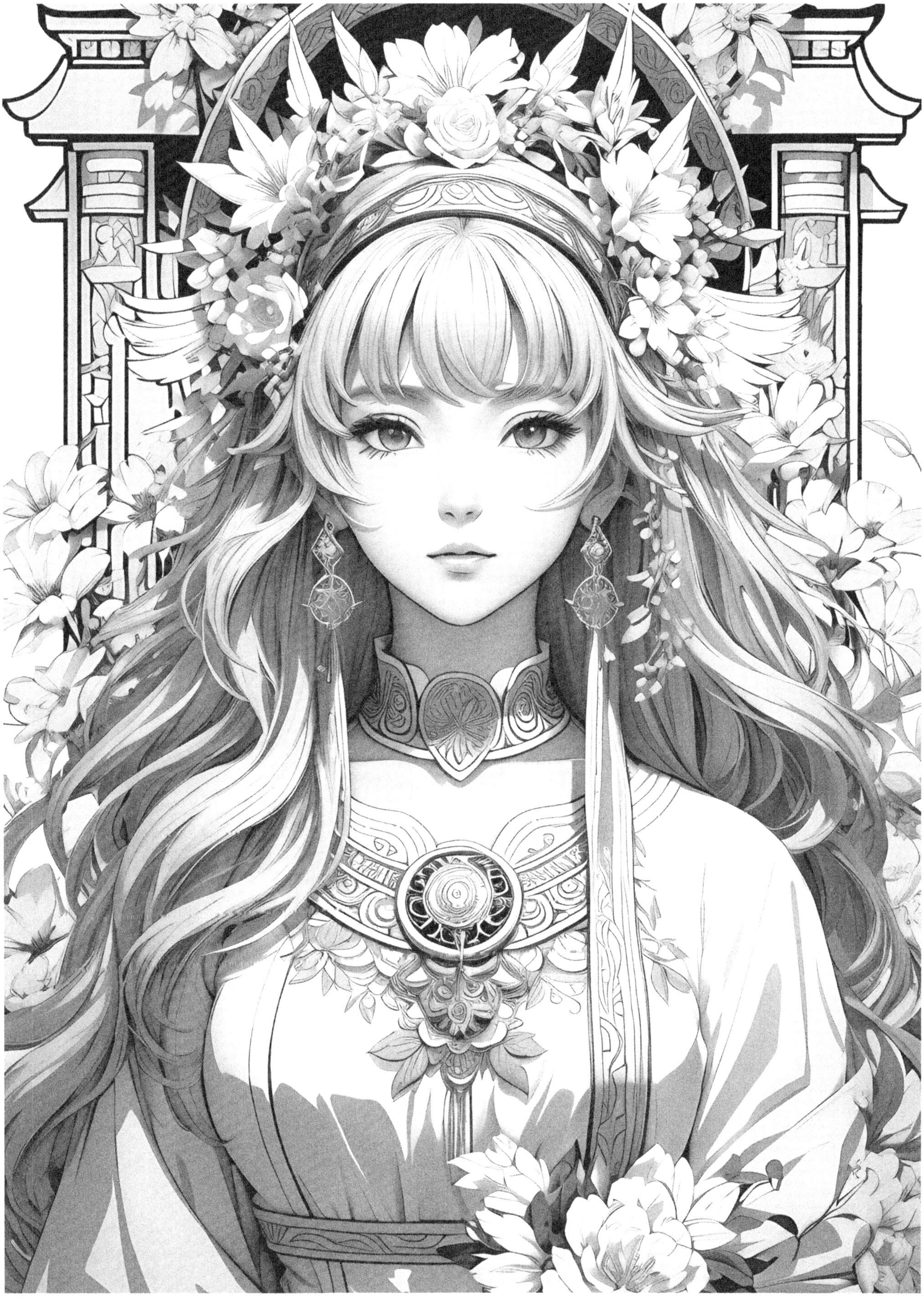

Printed by Amazon Italia Logistica S.r.l.
Torrazza Piemonte (TO), Italy

60095336R00065